Other Hamlyn titles in this series you will enjoy:

The Hamlyn Book of Ghosts	ISBN 0 600 34053 8
The Hamlyn Book of Horror	ISBN 0 600 34558 0
The Hamlyn Book of Mysteries	ISBN 0 600 36420 8

The Hamlyn Book of Monsters

Daniel Farson

HAMLYN
London · New York · Sydney · Toronto

Acknowledgements

Ardea, London: Kenneth W. Fink 100-101, Peter Green 33 inset, Arthur Hayward 48-49; Associated Newspapers Group Ltd, London 41 top left, 41 top centre, 41 top right; BBC Hulton Picture Library, London 15 bottom, 94, 95; BBC Photographs, London endpapers, 100 inset, 124 inset, 124-125, 126-127, 127 top right, 127 centre right, 127 bottom right; Bruce Coleman Limited, Uxbridge: Alain Compost 28; Canon Cotter 68; "The Daily Telegraph" Colour Library, London: Chris Holland 120, Homer Sykes 25 top; Daniel Farson 99; Fortean Picture Library, Montgomery 21 top inset, 21 bottom inset, 33, 57 right; Fortean Picture Library: Loren Coleman 77 top right, René Dahinden 36 top left, 73 bottom right, 76 left, M. P. Meaney 36 bottom right, Nicholas Witchell 42; Sonia Halliday Photographs, Weston Turville 24-25 bottom; Hamlyn Group Picture Library 55 right, 65; Michael Holford, Loughton 24 top; The Kobal Collection, London 8, 20-21, 26-27 bottom, 27 top, 73 top right, 80, 104, 105, 108-109, 110-111, 112-113, 115, 116-117, 119 top, 128-129, 130-131, 132-133, 133 top right, 134 top, 136; London Express News and Features Services 83; The Mansell Collection, London 53 right, 78-79 bottom, 79 top, 87 right, 135; Mary Evans Picture Library, London 10, 14, 15 top, 85; Operation Drake, London 30-31, 31 right; Gary Parfitt, Bath title page, 106-107, 111 inset, 116 top, 116 bottom, 134 bottom left; Rev. R. C. Poston 58; Ann Ronan Picture Library, Taunton 34-35; Royal Geographical Society, London 73 left inset; Tony Stone Associates Ltd, London 24 centre, 44-45 bottom; Syndication International Library, London 45 top right

Illustrated by
Victor Ambrus, Oliver Frey, Douglas Hall, John James, Ivan Lapper, *David Lewis Artists* (Robert Adams, Mike Codd), Tony Masero

Cover illustration by
Oliver Frey

Dedication
For James and Jeremy Thompson of Appledore

Published 1984 by
The Hamlyn Publishing Group Limited
London · New York · Sydney · Toronto
Astronaut House, Feltham, Middlesex, England

ISBN 0 600 36461 5
Printed in Italy

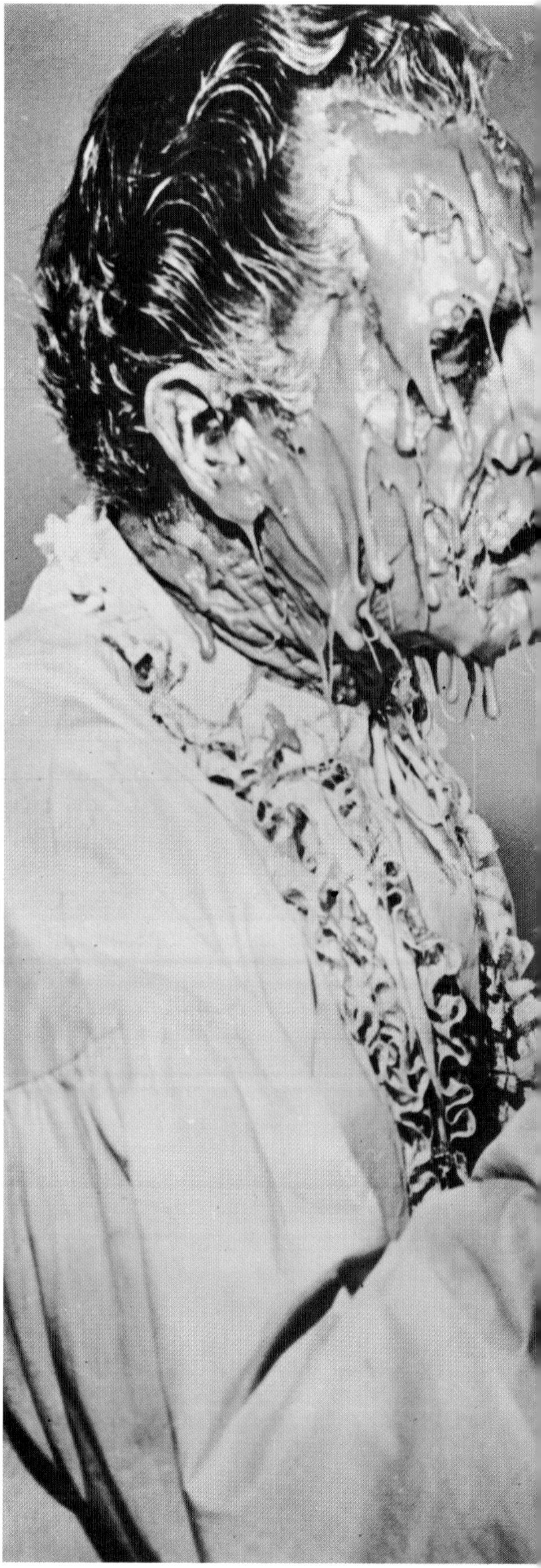

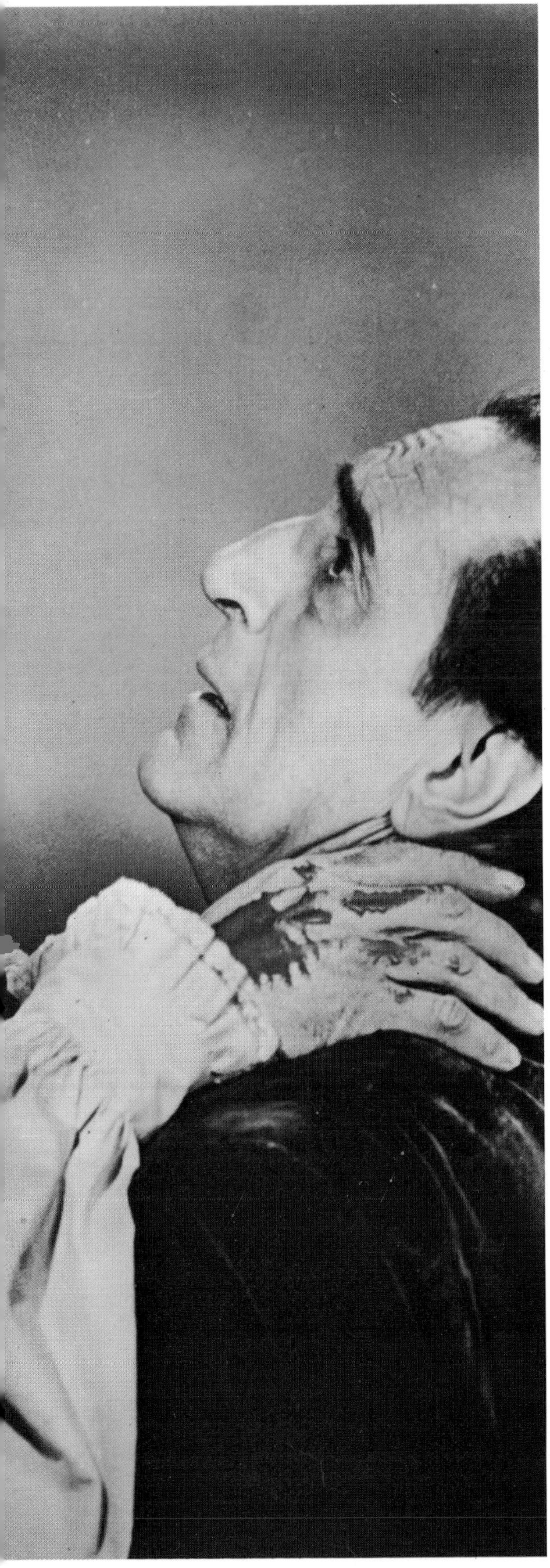

Contents

What is a Monster

One man's monster is another man's friend. Or at least another monster's. A hippopotamus probably does not look monstrous to another hippopotamus.

A monster is something different which we do not understand. If you had never seen a horse before it might look frightening – as it did to the Aztecs when the Spanish invaded Mexico – but we know better.

Monsters can be a state of mind, or symbols of good and evil, like fire-breathing dragons. Monsters can be mythical, like the Minotaur.

Monsters can be mistakes. When the early Elizabethan explorers returned from Africa with wild stories of monstrous men with beards, and heads growing beneath their shoulders, they had glimpsed gorillas in the jungle. What did the gorillas think of them?

Monsters can be as huge as gorillas – but gorillas are quite gentle whereas the deadly scorpion is small.

Monsters are fun! As the world becomes increasingly uniform, the idea of something so threatening is exciting. The Germans have a word for it – *schadenfreude* – which means the thrill we get from reading about horrible things which are happening to other people while we are safely tucked up in bed. We like to hear about monsters which we have little chance of meeting for ourselves. But are we so safe after all? Who knows what lurks out there?

Monsters are all around us. They appear in the most unexpected shapes and sizes as you will see.

Monsters can be *us*!

Daniel Farson

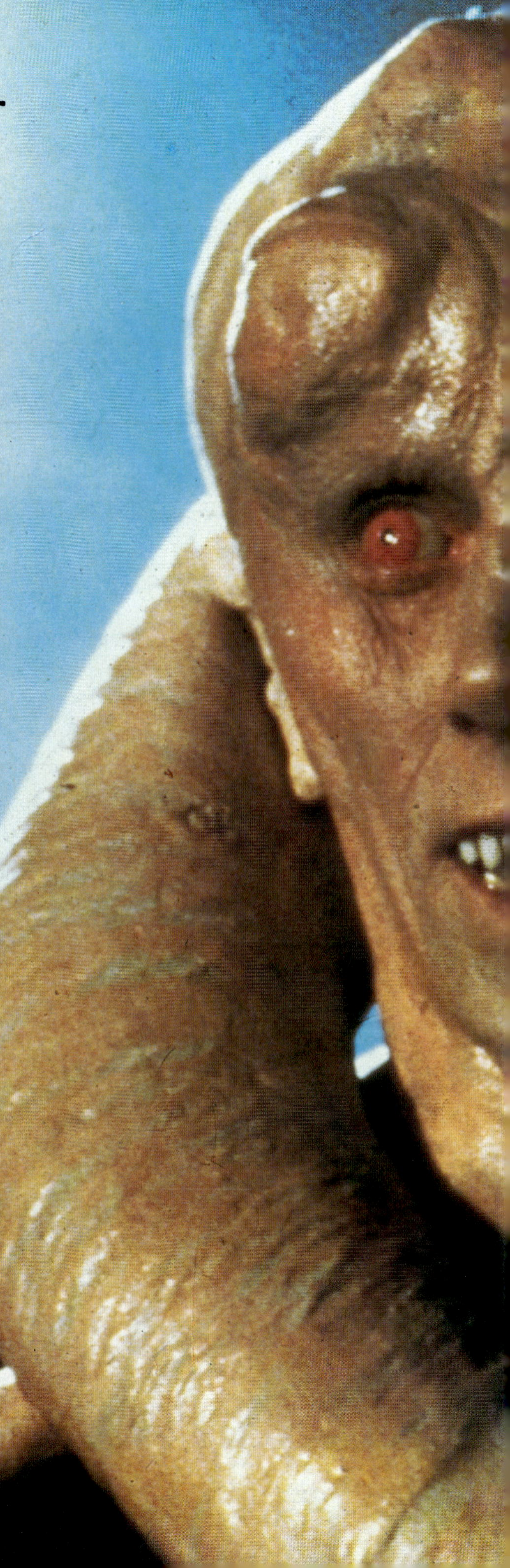

Chapter One

What Went Wrong with the World?

There is no reason for saying that the survival of some types of Mesozoic dinosaurs is impossible.

Dr Monard

Once upon a time the earth belonged to the monsters. Of course they didn't seem monstrous to each other, but today we think of prehistoric monsters as being strange creatures – huge, lumbering dinosaurs advancing on their hind legs, over 7 m (25 ft) high and sometimes over 13 m (45 ft) long. Though they ruled the earth for 140 million years, their fossils were only identified two hundred years ago, hardly a blink in time. It was the British palaeontologist (or person who studies fossils), Sir Richard Owen, who discovered the immense fossilized bones of land-living, egg-laying reptiles and gave them their name by joining two Greek words together – *deinous* which means 'terrible', and *sauros* which means 'lizard' – making *dinosaur*, or 'terrible lizard'.

These monsters were the kings of the earth. The *Brontosaurus*, whose skeleton was discovered in Wyoming, USA, in 1898, caused a sensation when the bones were assembled in the American Museum in New York – it was 4·5 m (15 ft) high and 20 m (67 ft) long. The *Brachiosaurus* was even longer – 30 m (nearly 100 ft) in length. Its weight was equal to that of fifteen elephants, only surpassed by the blue whale which is still alive.

Surprisingly, both these ferocious looking monsters were vegetarian. You might wonder how we can tell, 200 million years later – this is because remnants of food were found in their fossilized stomachs. However, many of the monsters became meat-eaters, killing for food.

These included *Tyrannosaurus Rex*, whose name means 'tyrant king', which is very appropriate. It stood on its hind legs with a vast head, fearsome jaws and sword-like teeth. But its front legs were little more than flippers, and because of its size the tyrant king was a clumsy creature, menaced by smaller, faster reptiles who stole its eggs and ate them. A complete skeleton was found by Dr Barnum Brown in South Dakota, USA, and the skilful reconstruction towers over visitors today in the American Museum in New York while fossilized bones are displayed in the Dinosaur National Monument in Utah.

The *Triceratops* was a lumbering rhinoceros-like monster with three horns, two over each of its eyes and one over its nose. It looks aggressive, but the horns were mainly used for bending down the branches of trees so it could nibble at the leaves.

Sir Richard Owen, the British scientist who discovered dinosaur bones.

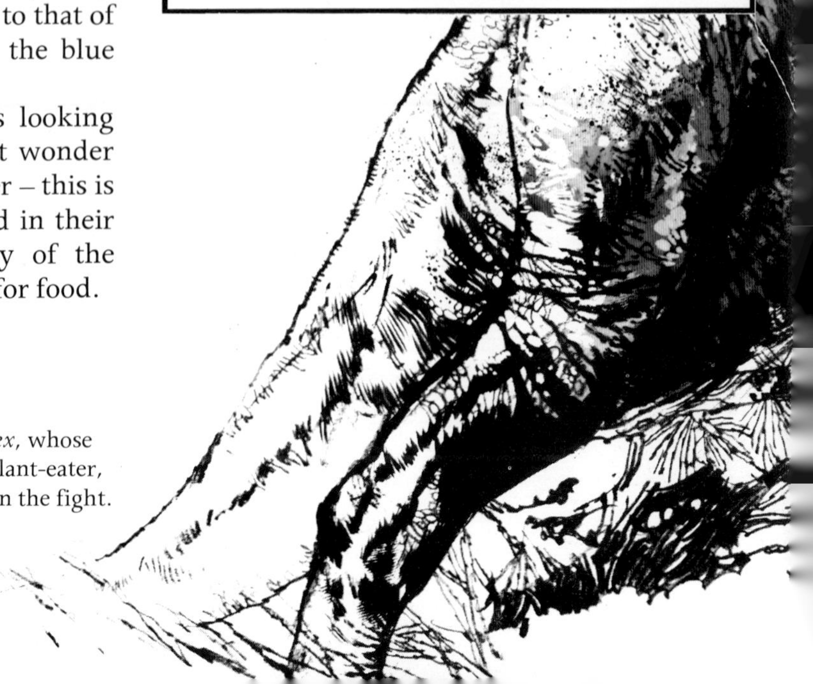

The meat-eating dinosaur *Tyrannosaurus Rex*, whose name means 'tyrant king', battles with the plant-eater, *Triceratops*. *Tyrannosaurus Rex* is likely to win the fight.

These were some of the monsters which roamed the earth in prehistoric times. The water was dominated by a series of sea-reptiles evolving over millions of years from tiny living organisms, like jellified worms, to the gigantic, amphibious *Ichthyostegid*. Ichthyosaur means 'fish-reptile' – living in swamps, cold-blooded, scaly and waterproof, these animals resembled four-legged fish and were able to adapt and survive when the climate became hotter. Their eggs were not laid but hatched inside the body.

The *Plesiosaurus* was a marine reptile resembling the Loch Ness Monster as we think of him or her today, with a long neck up to 6 m (20 ft), a tiny head, huge body, short tail and four paddle-like flippers. It used its neck like a whip, swinging round to catch its prey.

While these monsters ruled the land and water, *Pterodactyls* flew above them, similar reptiles but with wings which let them glide over the earth. Their bodies were surprisingly light because of their hollow bones.

The *Quetzalcoatlus* was a flying dragon with a 9-m (30-ft) wingspan. It rose with currents of warm air rising from the steaming earth, gliding as it floated in search of food, falling out of the sky like a stone when it found its victim or spotted a carcass. Fossils of *Quetzalcoatlus* were unearthed in Texas in 1975.

These were the most powerful of the monsters whose rule suddenly came to an end 65 million years ago. What happened? What went wrong with the world?

An immense catastrophe must have overwhelmed the earth and every living thing on it, but as human beings had not yet been created no record was left to hint at what this might have been. It happened so long ago that people

can only guess, but the various theories suggest one likely answer: a massive explosion caused by something from outside, like a vast hurtling asteroid 10 km (6 miles) wide; or from the earth itself, like a huge volcanic eruption. Such an explosion would have raised a cloud of dust cutting off the vital sunlight, so that the plants and plankton shrivelled and died.

Deprived of their food, the plant-eating dinosaurs would have perished, and when these had gone the carnivorous monsters would have lost their main source of meat. In a few years the earth would have turned into a desert of brown withered plants strewn with the bones of the great monsters, especially the largest, which would have proved the weakest. As they say of heavyweight boxers, 'The bigger they are, the harder they fall,' and the massive monsters would have been the most vulnerable. They would have been unable to escape their smaller enemies, some of which might only have been about 1 m (3 ft) tall, who could adapt to new conditions. These smaller creatures had better vision and a developing intelligence; and claws to help them catch other mammals even smaller than themselves for food, and survive.

This is probably how the prehistoric monsters came to an end. If the explanation strikes you as too simple, a recent example proves how easily the sunlight could have been shut off from the earth's surface. In April 1983 a reconnaissance U-2 plane reported a 'monster' cloud caused by the eruption of the El Chinchonal volcano in Mexico on 29 March. This cloud was 27 400 m (90 000 ft) high and stretched 20 900 km (13 000 miles) across the Pacific Ocean. From a satellite, this resembled a grey-white haze 140 times thicker than the dense cloud released by the volcanic eruption of Mount St Helens, Washington, USA, in 1980, which is known to have cut off light and affected the temperature below.

When you consider that most people have never heard of El Chinchonal, let alone its recent eruption, imagine the devastation released 65 million years ago by an explosion releasing ten million times such energy.

History shows us the devastation which comparatively small eruptions have caused in the past. Around 1500 BC the eruption of the volcano on the island of Santorini in the Mediterranean probably caused a tidal wave which

View of *The Lost World*. Two large *Plateosaurus* feeding; a small carnivore, Coelophysis, hunts nearby; and a phytosaur swims in the lake.

swept towards Crete, 100 km (60 miles) to the south, and overwhelmed Knossos, the centre of the Minoan civilization. In 1883, the Krakatoa eruption in Indonesia caused a drop in temperature for several years over a wide area. The 1912 eruption of Mount Katmai in Alaska was thought to be responsible for the cold, rainy summers as far away as Britain for the next two years. It only needs a slight reduction in the sun's energy to upset the entire balance of our climate, by preventing the rays of light from reaching us and stopping growth.

You can picture what probably happened: nature slowly dying, like the running-down of a record-player due to an electrical failure, with the great dinosaurs starting to slow down and fall from hunger, finally crumbling into dust. The question remains: did any of them escape?

Did any prehistoric monster survive?

Experts claim that no prehistoric monster survived the great catastrophe, and if you think of the continual process of breeding needed to sustain a species through a period lasting 65 million years, their argument seems logical. But experts are frequently wrong. After all, if someone had predicted a few hundred years ago that human beings would land on the moon and be watched by people on earth through a box in the corner of the room, they would have been considered mad, been locked up or burnt.

The true expert admits that he or she does not know everything.

It is possible that places and species exist, even today, of which we have no inkling.

Explorers find a lost world in South America

For several days the explorers had made their way through dense vegetation, led by two British professors Challenger and Summerlee, with six natives, on the expedition up the Amazon. A young journalist called Ed Malone described what happened after they made camp at the foot of an immensely high plateau. Suddenly something swooped over them like an aeroplane:

> 'The whole group of us were covered for an instant by a canopy of leathery wings and I had a momentary vision of a long, snake-like neck, a fierce red greedy eye, and a great snapping beak, filled, to my amazement, with little gleaming teeth. The next instant it was gone – and so was our dinner. A huge black shadow, 20 ft [6 m] across, skimmed up into the air; for an instant the monster wings blotted out the stars, and then it vanished over the brow of the cliff above us.'

Maple White's imaginary illustration from Conan Doyle's *The Lost World*.

This was the expedition's first glimpse of a *Pterodactyl*, confirming the rumours that the plateau above them had been cut off from time. When they managed to reach the top, they found a valley alive with the terrifying winged monsters of the past – a rookery of *Pterodactyls*:

> 'All the bottom area round the water-edge was alive with their young ones, and with hideous mothers brooding upon their leathery, yellowish eggs. From this crawling, flapping mass of obscene reptilian life came the shocking clamour which filled the air and the . . . horrible, musty odour which turned us sick. But above, perched each upon its own stone, tall, grey, withered, more like dead and dried specimens than actual living creatures, sat the horrible males, absolutely motionless save for the rolling of their red eyes or an occasional snap of their rat-trap beaks as a dragonfly went past them. Their huge, membranous wings were closed by folding their fore-arms, so that they sat like gigantic old women, wrapped in hideous web-coloured shawls, and with their ferocious heads protruding above them. Large and small, not less than a thousand of these filthy creatures lay in the hollow before us.'

Above: A photograph of the imaginary members of Conan Doyle's exploring party was published in early editions of the book to make people think the story was real. From left to right: Ed Malone, Prof Summerlee, Prof Challenger and Lord John Roxton.

Below: Sir Arthur Conan Doyle, who wrote the exciting adventure story *The Lost World*.

After warding off an attack by the *Pterodactyls*, the expedition met other monsters, such as a giant toad with 'a warty, leprous skin and a loose mouth all beslobbered with fresh blood', but the most shocking encounter took place when the journalist climbed to the top of a tall tree to overlook the land, and found himself staring at something so surprising he almost fell to the ground:

> 'A face was gazing into mine – at a distance of only a foot or two [under 1 m]. The creature that owned it had been crouching behind the parasite, and had looked round it at the same instant that I did. It was a human face – or at least it was far more human than any monkey's that I have ever seen.'

Though the expedition was prepared for evidence of prehistoric monsters, they had overlooked the possibility of prehistoric human beings. In this they were historically correct, for humans did not yet exist in the Jurassic period, when these prehistoric monsters were around, so humans and beasts never lived together, and this gives the game away. Far from being reports of a real expedition, they are sheer fantasy, from the imagination of Sir Arthur Conan Doyle (1859-1930) in his novel *The Lost World*. This is one of the most splendid monster books of all time, though Conan Doyle is better known for his creation of the great detective, Sherlock Holmes.

First published in 1912, *The Lost World* is a first-rate 'yarn' with Conan Doyle's zest for adventure and sense of fun fulfilling the modest objective stated at the beginning:

'I have wrought my simple plan
If I give one hour of joy
To the boy, who's half a man,
Or the man who's half a boy.'

An expedition into Central Africa

'Its vast jungles and swamplands have been bypassed in all the modern hubbub,' wrote the explorer Ivan Sanderson in *More 'Things'* (1969). 'Thousands of locations that were fairly well known 50 years ago have now been virtually lost. The mere size of the place is quite beyond comprehension to those who have not visited it, so it is quite useless to suggest that there is not room in it for all manner of things as yet unknown.'

The *Lost World* expedition met horrible monsters, including *Pterodactyls* and a warty, leprous toad.

Sanderson wrote from first-hand experience after travelling by canoe along a remote river in West Africa in 1932. Taken by the currents, Sanderson and a fellow-explorer entered a deep gorge with sheer cliffs and black caves on either side. Suddenly there was a roar (and this is fact not fiction):

> 'The most terrible noise I have heard, short of an oncoming earthquake or the explosion of an aerial torpedo at close range, suddenly burst from one of the big caves on my right . . . I started to paddle like mad but I was swept close to the entrance of the cave from which the noise had come.
>
> 'Something enormous rose out of the water, turning it to sherry-coloured foam, and then, again roaring, plunged below. This "thing" was shiny black and was the *head* of something, shaped like a seal but flattened from above to below. It was about the size of a full-grown hippopotamus – this head I mean. We exited from the gorge at a speed that would have done credit to the Harvard Eight . . .'

Local Africans knew the creature as a M'Koo: 'These animals lived there all the time, they told us, and that is why there were no crocodiles or hippos in that river. But, they went on, M'Koo does not eat flesh, but only the big liana fruits and juicy herbiage by the river.'

Could the American naturalist have been mistaken? He was the first to admit he was never sure of what he had seen and this doubt is more convincing than the absolute certainty of most reports. Sanderson's reliability has been vouched for by the zoologist Dr Bernard Heuvelmans in his book entitled *On the Track of Unknown Animals*, while Angus Hall, another expert, refers to Sanderson's experience in *Monsters and Mythic Beasts* (1975) and reaches an interesting conclusion of his own – that smaller dinosaurs might have survived needing less food. 'Were they able to find a better area and slowly adapt to changes?' he asks. 'Sanderson knew that there had been "very curious goings-on in Africa for more than a century".'

The expedition of Captain Von Stein

Angus Hall refers to the expedition led by Capt Von Stein in 1913 when the German government sent him to explore the mountains of the Cameroons, Central Africa, and prepare a survey map of the area. The outbreak of the First World War interrupted this, but Von Stein recorded a sensational encounter in a private manuscript. Though he was a hard-headed soldier, he became interested in the reports of a 'mysterious thing' which lived in one of the rivers, and though his sources were different they all described the same features which made them sound convincing.

At last the 'thing' surfaced in the Sanaga River which Von Stein's expedition was exploring for the first time:

> '... brownish-grey colour with a smooth skin, its size approximately that of an elephant.... It is said to have a long and very flexible neck and only one tooth, but a very long one; some say it is a horn. A few spoke about a long muscular tail like that of an alligator. Canoes coming near it are said to be doomed; the animal is said to attack the vessels at once and to kill the crews, but without eating the bodies. The creature is said to have lived in the caves that have been washed out by the river... It is said to climb the shore even at daytime in search of food; its diet is said to be entirely vegetable.'

In every respect the description fits a herbivorous prehistoric monster like a type of *Brontosaurus* – and this is only one report of many.

In 1909 two Germans, who supplied wild animals to zoos, heard of a creature half-elephant and half-dragon with a single horn like a rhinoceros. They were so convinced this was a dinosaur that they financed an expedition to capture it – without success.

In 1919, at the time of Von Stein's expedition, *The Times*, London, reported that an 'extraordinary monster' had been sighted in the Belgian Congo (now the Congo). It had charged an engineer called Lepage who was building a railway. Lepage fired at the beast and then fled, with the animal in pursuit until it lost interest.

Boats coming near the 'mysterious thing' are said to be doomed.

The breathless Lepage turned round and studied the monster through his binoculars. It bore a striking resemblance to the three-horned dinosaur known as the *Triceratops* – it was 7 m (24 ft) in length with a long pointed snout adorned with tusks like horns, and a short horn above the nostrils. The front feet were like those of a horse, and the hind hoofs were cloven. There was a scaly lump on the monster's shoulder.

With unusual foresight, the government of the country listed the monster as a 'relic of antiquity'. They said it was not to be harmed, although it had rampaged through a village, killing a number of natives, and charged headlong into a train (which it might have mistaken for a rival monster), killing several of the passengers. The Smithsonian Institute in America offered three million dollars if anyone could produce the monster dead or alive, but the reward was never claimed.

Of course these reports could have been fakes or genuine mistakes. The split-second glimpse of a malformed rhinoceros could well defy a simple explanation if seen at dusk – light can play the strangest tricks, especially on water. However, an eminent Swiss zoologist called Dr Monard, who accompanied another 'dinosaur' expedition in 1932, to Angola, is prepared to believe that such things are possible.

The great dinosaur race

The search goes on. In November 1981, the London *Daily Express* reported 'The great race to catch a dinosaur' between a biology professor from Chicago University, Dr Roy Mackal, and a Californian space scientist, Herman Regusters. The two men decided to investigate sightings of monsters in Lake Tumba, north of Brazzaville, the capital of the Congo, West Central Africa.

They started together then disagreed and followed separate routes. Mackal's team took an amphibious plane to Lake Tele, but low cloud prevented a landing and they had to start again using canoes, 'paddling up the River Congo (Zaire) in serious and costly earnestness.' Herman Regusters, the 47-year-old son of a black missionary, resigned from the Pasadena jet propulsion laboratory where he worked and travelled with his wife and a television cameraman.

Though Mackal was financed by the National Geographic Society and a Texan millionaire, both men knew that the commercial profits would be stupendous if they returned with proof of the monster, quite apart from the international fame.

No reward has been claimed, but Mackal returned more convinced than ever that such monsters *do* exist after seeing tracks which could have been made by a giant reptile – 'the branches were broken 1·5 to 2 m (5 to 6 ft) above the ground. No known crocodile is that large.' Mackal and his colleague, James Powell, still believe that a monster with a long neck and tail, the size of an elephant, might exist in the deep lakes of the Congo and Central Africa. After showing various photographs to the natives who claim to have seen it, they have reached the conclusion that the description is closest to that of a dinoaur – and dinosaurs are supposed to be extinct.

'The existence of a large saurian [dinosaur or lizard] descended from the reptiles of the Mesozoic era is by no means theoretically impossible. Though every continent has been crossed and recrossed, most travellers follow much the same track, and there are still holes in the net to be explored. There have been several reports that some kind of *Brontosaurus* survives, and several expeditions have even gone to look for it; the fact that they failed may merely prove that this prehistoric beast is very rare or that it lives in country as inaccessible as the great swamps.

'There are some reasons, based on the history of the continents and the great reptiles, for thinking that they could survive . . . While it is not scientific to be too credulous, it is no better to be incredulous; and there is no reason for saying that the survival of some types of Mesozoic saurians is impossible.'

Chapter Two

Dragons and other Mythical Beasts

I waited for him to give way, but his only response was to lower his head, puff out his throat and hiss.

Lyall Watson

Tales of dragons are the most enduring of the monster myths. A dragon is described by the Oxford dictionary as 'a mythical monster like a crocodile or snake with wings and claws and often breathing fire' – but even though it is a mythical beast, the dragon also has a deep symbolic importance and many dragon festivals are held today.

The dragon is highly adaptable, all things to all people. In ancient times it represented the forces of nature, the change from day to night, and summer to winter, with the slaying of the dragon interpreted as the end of the year.

In the East, the dragon has been honoured as a kindly god, and Chinese Emperors used to sit on dragon-shaped thrones and travel by dragon-headed boats.

In the West, the dragon has been the symbol of evil, a monster who guards a rare treasure or has captured a beautiful girl, which is why it has to be slain.

St George and the dragon

This is the most famous dragon legend of all. It tells of a fearless warrior called George of Lydda who was riding through Libya in North Africa to confront the king and plead for the lives of some Christian slaves. On his way he learned of a monstrous dragon which lurked in a swamp outside the nearby city of Silene. The local people were so terrified of it that they had sacrificed their own sons and daughters in the hope of satisfying the monster, which was

Tales of dragons are the most enduring of the monster myths. Shown here is a scene from the film *Dragonslayer*.

Top: The fearless warrior, George of Lydda, shown here slaying the dragon in a 16th-century woodcut by Albrecht Dürer.

Bottom: A dragon-slaying carved on an early 16th-century bench end in Crowcombe Church, Somerset, England.

scorching them to death with its fiery breath, until only a few girls were left. In their desperation, the people drew lots and the king's beautiful daughter, Princess Sabra, had just been chosen as the next victim and was now at the mercy of the monster.

George of Lydda tracked down the creature and charged it with his spear, forcing it down on the ground. The princess quickly slipped her belt around the dragon's neck, and they were able to drag the creature into the city of Silene where the citizens rejoiced and accepted the Christian faith in gratitude. With one foot on the monster's body, George of Lydda cut off the dragon's head. He then married the king's beautiful daughter.

Susa No and the eight-headed monster

This story is told in one of the earliest poems ever written. A brave young man called Susa No came across the Emperor of Japan who was weeping because his daughter was about to be sacrificed to a sea monster with eight heads. Susa No thought up a plan. He built a house with eight roofless rooms around a central, covered square. He tempted the monster in by placing an open barrel of saki (a potent alcoholic Japanese drink) inside each room. Then he dressed in the princess's clothes and climbed on to the central roof, looking over the side. From here his reflection fell into one of the barrels. The dragon saw it and mistook it for the princess so it dived in, swallowing all the saki. As Susa No moved clockwise round the central roof, the serpent pursued each reflection, emptying each barrel of the saki until it had drunk the lot. It was so giddy that Susa No had little difficulty in jumping down and cutting off the monster's eight heads. In the true tradition of such stories, he was rewarded with marriage to the princess and became the new king.

Bellerophon and the stinking Chimera

Apart from their poisonous bite, all dragons have one thing in common – a really foul, fiery breath. Significantly, the huge anaconda snakes found in Sri Lanka and South America today are known for their stinking breath as well. In Greek mythology the Chimera was undoubtedly a form of dragon, though it had the head of a lion, the body of a goat, a serpent's tail and vile breath.

Bellerophon, the hero of Corinth and the Son of Poseidon, God of the Sea, was given the task of slaying the Chimera. He worked out a plan of exceptional cunning. After slipping a golden bridle over the winged horse Pegasus, which he had captured and tamed, he rode into the sky above the monstrous Chimera. He pelted it with

Susa No slaying the eight-headed monster and saving the daughter of the Emperor of Japan.

arrows, then finally fixed a lump of lead on the tip of his lance, thrusting this straight into the monster's mouth. As he hoped, the Chimera's breath was so hot that it melted the lead. This ran down into the creature's stomach, burning it to death.

Did you know that you can still find the Chimera today? Sailors can see the red, fiery glow as they sail past Mount Phoenix on the south-west coast of Turkey. In fact the Chimera is a large hole in the ground among the surrounding woods above the ancient town of Olympus which has belched forth fire for centuries. The 'unceasing flame' is like a small volcanic crater, little bigger than an oven, where Turkish shepherds used to cook their meat. However, legend has it that if they were trying to cook food which had been stolen it remained raw and could not be roasted.

It has been suggested that the legendary monster was a combination of the lions, goats and snakes which lived in these mountains, together with the flame, but it is more likely that the Turkish Chimera was named after the legend which dates back to the Iliad:

> 'Chimera the unconquerable . . . of divine birth was she and not of men, in front a lion, and behind a serpent, and the midst a goat; and she breathed dread fierceness of blazing fire.'

The slaying of the Minotaur

If St George represents virtue while the dragon is the symbol of everything bad, the story of the Cretan Minotaur can be seen as another version of the legendary combat between man and beast.

When King Minos ruled the island of Crete, he boasted that the gods would grant him anything he asked for in return for the traditional sacrifice of an animal. Usually this sacrifice was a goat, but after Minos built an altar to Poseidon (the God of the Sea, also known as Neptune, who stirred up storms with his trident), Minos prayed that a bull should emerge from the water and, sure enough, this happened. A great white bull swam to the shore, but it was such a magnificent beast that Minos could not bear to see it killed in the sacrificial ritual and sent it secretly to join his own herds, sacrificing another bull instead.

However, the gods cannot be deceived so easily, and Poseidon took the deception as a personal insult, plotting a cruel revenge. He encouraged Pasiphae, the wife of Minos, to fall in love with the animal. She did, but the bull took little notice of her until Pasiphae persuaded Daedalus, the brilliant engineer at the Palace of Knossos, to design a hollow wooden cow in which she could hide. The model was built on wheels and was pushed into the meadow. It was so beautifully constructed that the bull fell in love with it. The result of this odd match was the birth of the monstrous Minotaur: half-man and half-bull.

Minos was appalled when he discovered what had happened, and he asked an oracle how to avoid the scandal and disgrace it would cause. He was told to command Daedalus to design a maze underneath the palace. From then on, Minos spent most of his life with the monster and Pasiphae, concealed at the heart of the Labyrinth where no one could find them.

Just as boys and girls were sacrificed to the dragon outside Silene, Minos left orders that seven Athenian youths and seven maidens should be sent from Greece to Knossos every year to feed the Minotaur. This caused the parents of Athens such great grief that the hero Theseus offered himself as one of the sacrificial young men. When his ship arrived at Crete, Ariadne (the daughter of Pasiphae and Minos) fell in love with Theseus the moment she saw him. She offered her help in killing the Minotaur (her half-brother) if Theseus would agree to marry her and take her back to Athens. Theseus had fallen in love with her too, and agreed readily. Ariadne then gave him a ball of twine, telling him how to unravel it through the maze until he reached the place where the Minotaur was hidden.

Theseus followed the twine down the labyrinthine passages until he found the sleeping monster. He seized it by the hair and stabbed it to death with a sword given him secretly by Ariadne. At last the bull was sacrificed to Poseidon. Theseus was able to escape from the intricate maze by following the twine back until he emerged in the palace, where Ariadne and the Athenian youths were waiting for him. Racing back to their ship on the coast, they made their escape and Theseus set sail to new adventures.

These myths of dragons and minotaurs may seem like fairy stories, but they should never be dismissed as mere fantasy. Like all the old legends, they symbolize something deeper.

The union of the white bull and Queen Pasiphae may have signified the ritual marriage between a moon-priestess, wearing the horns of a cow, and the king, with the mask of a bull – representing the coming together of the moon and the sun. Such masks were a common feature in ancient rites.

In the same way, the search for the Minotaur could have symbolized an Athenian raid led by

Above: A Greek vase from the 6th century BC, which shows Theseus killing the Minotaur.

Below: These were the Queen's private rooms in the Palace of Knossos.

Below right: Celebrating the Chinese New Year.

Bottom: Bull-leaping frescoes at Knossos.

Theseus to assassinate King Minos. Theseus may have chased him down the corridors of the Palace of Knossos. There really was a maze in the palace, carefully laid out in the open mosaic floor. This was used for ritual dancing, which imitated the courtship of the partridge to begin with, though this was replaced by the cult of bull worship. The ball of twine could have symbolized the piece of string which kept the dancers apart. If you go to Greece today and watch the bouzouki dancers you will notice that this is still the practice, the dancers usually holding a handkerchief between them instead of string.

There is ample proof that the Cretans recognized the bull as a symbol of power, and this was confirmed when the archaeologist Sir Arthur Evans rediscovered the Palace of Knossos in the last century. Knossos had been submerged either by an earthquake or by the gigantic tidal wave which swept south from Santorini about 1450 BC, and oxen skulls were found in one of the buildings, probably sacrificed by the Cretans in an effort to appease the gods and avert the catastrophe. The bull is shown in the colourful frescoes unearthed by Evans, and one of the most famous depicts acrobatic young men leaping over the back of a bull. This was a sport of the time, as it is with young Spaniards today at the Festival of Pamplona, but the writer Robert Graves in his book *Greek Myths* (1955) has suggested that it was a religious rite as well, with the acrobats representing the planets. He adds: 'Four thousand years ago the Chimera can have seemed no more bizarre than any religious, heraldic or commercial emblem does today.'

This does not mean that the human sacrifices of the dragon-legends were purely imaginary; on the contrary, they probably took place at the start of the celebrations, according to Sir James Frazer (1854 to 1941) in his famous study of folklore, *The Golden Bough* (1890 to 1915): 'It would probably be a mistake to dismiss all these tales as pure inventions of the storyteller. Rather we suppose that they reflect a real custom of sacrificing girls or women to be the wives of water-spirits, who are very often conceived as great serpents or dragons.'

Today we are surrounded by symbols of dragons: the red dragon flies on the Welsh flag, while St George is the patron saint of England. This is the same Christian knight who slew the dragon at Silene and whose body was buried in the Holy Land, where his tomb became a sacred monument. Centuries later, the German Emperor Sigismond is supposed to have presented the heart of St George to King Henry V of England, which is how the order of the Knights of St George was founded at Windsor Castle.

The Chinese celebrate their new year with huge papier-mâché dragons made of wood and paper; while an ancient ceremony takes place every year in Burford in Oxfordshire, England, dating back to AD 752 when the town was divided across the boundaries of Wessex and Mercia (Oxfordshire and Gloucestershire today), and a battle took place between the two kingdoms to decide who should claim it. The Wessex soldiers led by Cathred defeated the Mercians on Midsummer's Eve. Models of a dragon (the emblem of Wessex) and a giant, which represents the might of Wessex, were paraded through the streets of Burford to celebrate the victory, and though the tradition died out around 1750 it was revived by the Burford Grammar School in 1971 as part of their quarter-centenary festival, and it still continues. The model of the dragon's head is mounted on wheels and the rest of the body, constructed by the school, covers thirty children who writhe and twist their way in serpentine style as they invade the town on Midsummer Eve, snorting out puffs of smoke. Though it attracts hundreds of people, it is one of the lesser-known of the dragon festivals today.

Dragons all around us

We think of the dragon as a mythical monster which never existed, except in the folk tales and legends of medieval Europe, and certainly does not do so today. But perhaps we are being too hasty . . .

The dictionary has compared a dragon to 'a crocodile or snake', and we only have to look at those reptiles which survived the cataclysm 65 million years ago to realize that dragon-like creatures are all around us: chameleons, lizards, the foul-smelling anacondas of Sri Lanka, and the iguanas of South America. Little wonder that film-makers like Hal Roach used them, blown-up to gigantic proportions, to represent prehistoric monsters in such films as *One Million BC* (1940).

It has been said that the first men who dared to venture into the interior of Central America, and came face to face with alligators for the first time, were so bewildered that when they returned they described them as dragons.

But could there have been other such monsters in the prehistoric past which were responsible for the legend of the dragon in the first place?

And if any of these monsters survived the cataclysm which destroyed the dinosaurs, is it just possible that a freak survivor exists today?

Prehistoric monsters in *One Million BC*.

Carole Landis and Victor Mature prepare to attack a giant monster, which is really an alligator blown up to gigantic proportions, in *One Million BC*.

The dragon in the Garden of Eden

These are true facts.

In 1912, the pilot of a pioneer plane crash-landed on the small island of Komodo, Indonesia. After he had been rescued he spoke of strange 'giant, lizard-like creatures' which had surrounded the wreckage of his plane. Most people laughed at his story, but Mr Ouwens, the curator of the Botanical Gardens on Java, was sufficiently impressed to ask the Dutch governor to authorize an official visit to the island.

Komodo lies in the middle of a chain of islands called the Sunda Islands in the Flores Sea, between Sumbawa, Bali and Java to the west, and Flores and Timor to the east. The islands are separated by straits where the currents are so fierce that few creatures would be able to cross them, which means that Komodo might have been cut off like Conan Doyle's lost world, with strange monsters like those reported by the pilot. It was certainly worth investigating.

Sure enough the Dutch official returned with the skin of a 2-m (7-ft) long creature, though some of the natives swore that the animals sometimes reached 9 m (30 ft) – the length probably growing with their anxiety to please. The skin might have been a hoax, but the curator had enough faith to launch a proper search for the monster, which was supposed to swallow up whole pigs and deer. A local rajah provided hunters and tracker dogs, and the explorers' enthusiasm was rewarded – the monsters did exist. Two were shot by a Dutch colonial soldier and brought back as evidence. The largest was almost 3 m (10 ft) long and the species was classified as a giant monitor lizard, becoming better known as the Komodo dragon.

The Komodo dragon is a true monster – or freak. Usually the monitor lizards reach a length of 60 to 90 cm (2 to 3 ft), but on Komodo without the usual carnivorous mammals to attack them, the reptiles have been able to develop to four times that length, into giants.

Lyall Watson, the author of *Supernature* (1973), claims Komodo dragons are now the largest lizards in the world: 'At up to 3·6 m (12 ft) in length, with a weight sometimes in excess of 130 kg (300 lb), they are easily the biggest reptiles to have stalked dry land since the age of the dinosaurs.'

Above: A Komodo Dragon: one of the biggest reptiles to have stalked dry land since the age of the dinosaur.

Right: 'Giant lizard-like creatures surrounded the wreckage of the pilot's plane'.

Lyall Watson has brought the pilot's story, first told seventy years ago, right up to date with sensational new evidence. Komodo remained isolated under the rule of the Sultan of Bima, Sumbawa, who disposed of criminals by the simple method of shipping them to the next island, Komodo. In this way, though it was not his intention, he might have supplied the dragons with food. Soon so many were reported that in 1928 he issued an order putting the island under special protection, and declaring it 'a wilderness area' which no one was allowed to visit without special permission.

One of the few people who did go there was David Attenborough, researching for a *Zoo Quest* programme for television, but Lyall Watson has provided the most detailed information of the dragon, even though his first sight of one was a disappointment. He had been lying on the edge of a ravine for three hours, looking down on the bait of a slaughtered goat which he had hung from a tree near the dragon's lair. Nothing had happened except that a lizard less than 0·6 m (2 ft) long had scrambled around the tree trunk. Watson was prepared to dismiss the stories of the giant monster and give up, when he heard a sound:

'There was a rustle of dry leaves a little way up the shady ravine and then, without further warning, a prehistoric monster stepped out into the sun. No photograph or film can capture the threat of a dragon in the flesh, in search of food. He stood with his broad head high, tasting the air with a forked yellow tongue, looking it seemed directly at me with a dark, cold, basilisk eye. His dusty, scarred skin was heavily scaled, hung in folds about his powerful neck, and was draped loosely over a body like a great trunk propped up clear of the ground by four muscular legs with long, clawed toes. When he moved, it was with surprising grace, throwing his enormous weight from side to side with a fluid reptilean movement of the hips.'

The dragon reached up with a lunge, ripped down the carcass of the goat, and tore it to pieces with his teeth. In a few minutes nothing was left but wisps of hair.

Learning all he could about the Komodo dragon, Watson discovered that they lay up to 30 eggs, in a deep hole. These take eight months to incubate, then 45-cm (18-in) long hatchlings emerge. By the time the dragons are six years old they have reached 1·5 m (5 ft) in length, but they have become less agile at tree-climbing and seize any food they can get their claws on, grabbing wild boar by their legs, or seizing deer from behind, away from the dangerous antlers. However, Watson also heard that a buffalo weighing 635 kg (1400 lb) was killed by a 2·1-m (7-ft) dragon.

Now it is claimed that they are adding human beings to their diet, after having sampled the early convicts. Most dragons keep out of the way of humans, but a few are braver and attack, such as 34 W, a monster which Lyall Watson encountered himself:

'I waited for him to give way, but his only response was to lower his head, puff out his throat and hiss. I backed off, but he kept on coming, walking stiff-legged, body held high off the ground. So I turned and ran.'

Watson was wise. Others have not been so lucky, including a 14-year-old boy whose family ran for help when he was attacked. When they returned with sticks they found that large chunks of flesh had been ripped from his back and the boy died from his wounds within an hour. On another occasion, a poacher fell ill and when his friends came back with medical aid, all they found were his legs.

In July 1974, a group of Swiss tourists came to the island on a wildlife tour, and a 78-year-old naturalist called Baron Von Reding decided to leave the group and make his way back to the boat slowly on his own. He was never seen again. All that has been found was his Hasselblad camera with a broken strap. Had 34 W struck again?

Having proved how real they are, the dragons have discouraged tourism and Komodo is becoming a lost world again – an 'Eden, complete with resident reptile', as Lyall Watson calls the island. It is easy to agree with his conclusion:

'These are terrible tales, though I must confess to a sneaking regard for the way these strange creatures resist the onward march of man.'

Postscript Another dragon-like creature was discovered as recently as 1981 on the expedition known as Operation Drake, a two-year voyage of boys and girls led by the British explorer Lieut-Col John Blashford-Snell. The young explorers found the longest lizard ever recorded, in the swamps of Papua New Guinea.

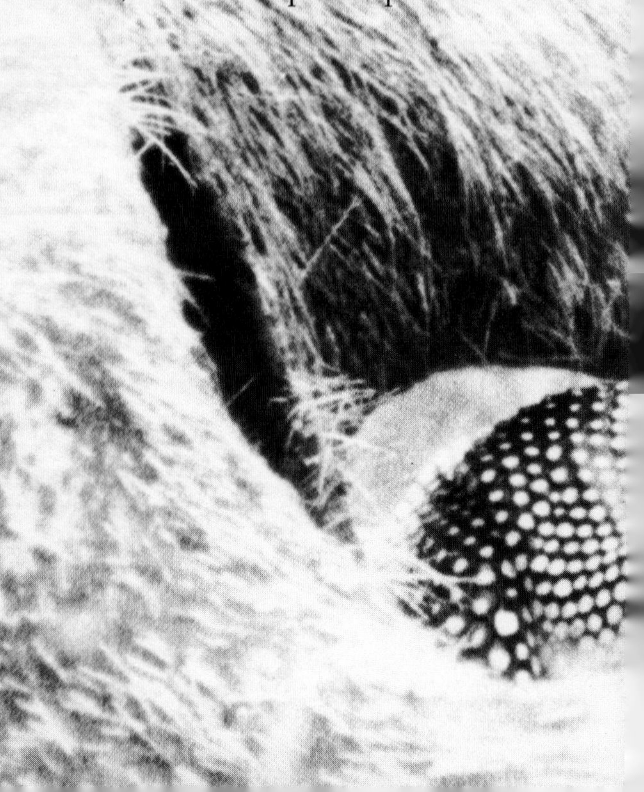

Described as a Salvadori dragon, it was 5·4 m (18 ft) long and was supposed to have killed a native with its claws and eaten him. As the previous Salvadori dragon was only 4·7 m (15·6 ft) long, listed in the *Guinness Book of Records* (1980), this makes Drake's dragon the latest and the largest, beating the Komodo dragon just mentioned.

Blashford-Snell's account is surprisingly similar to the fictitious reports of Ed Malone in *The Lost World*. 'It is a primeval area,' Blashford-Snell reported. 'Besides the lizards, we discovered a snake without eyes, and pimples on its skin instead of scales, which we have yet to identify; found 10-m (34-ft) sea-going crocodiles, and turtles with webbed feet.'

The discovery of a creature which has not yet been identified comes as a shock in the 1980s. In view of this, we cannot deny the possibility that monsters are lurking in remote corners of the world, of which we have no idea.

The fact that we have not seen them is no proof that they do not exist.

Arthur C Clarke, the well known science fiction writer, suggests there is 'room for a zoo-full of unknown animals in the forests of Africa,' and quotes the perfect answer to experts who claim that no unknown animals are left on earth:

> *'What is the most cunning of all*
> *the animals?*
> *That which no one has yet seen.'*

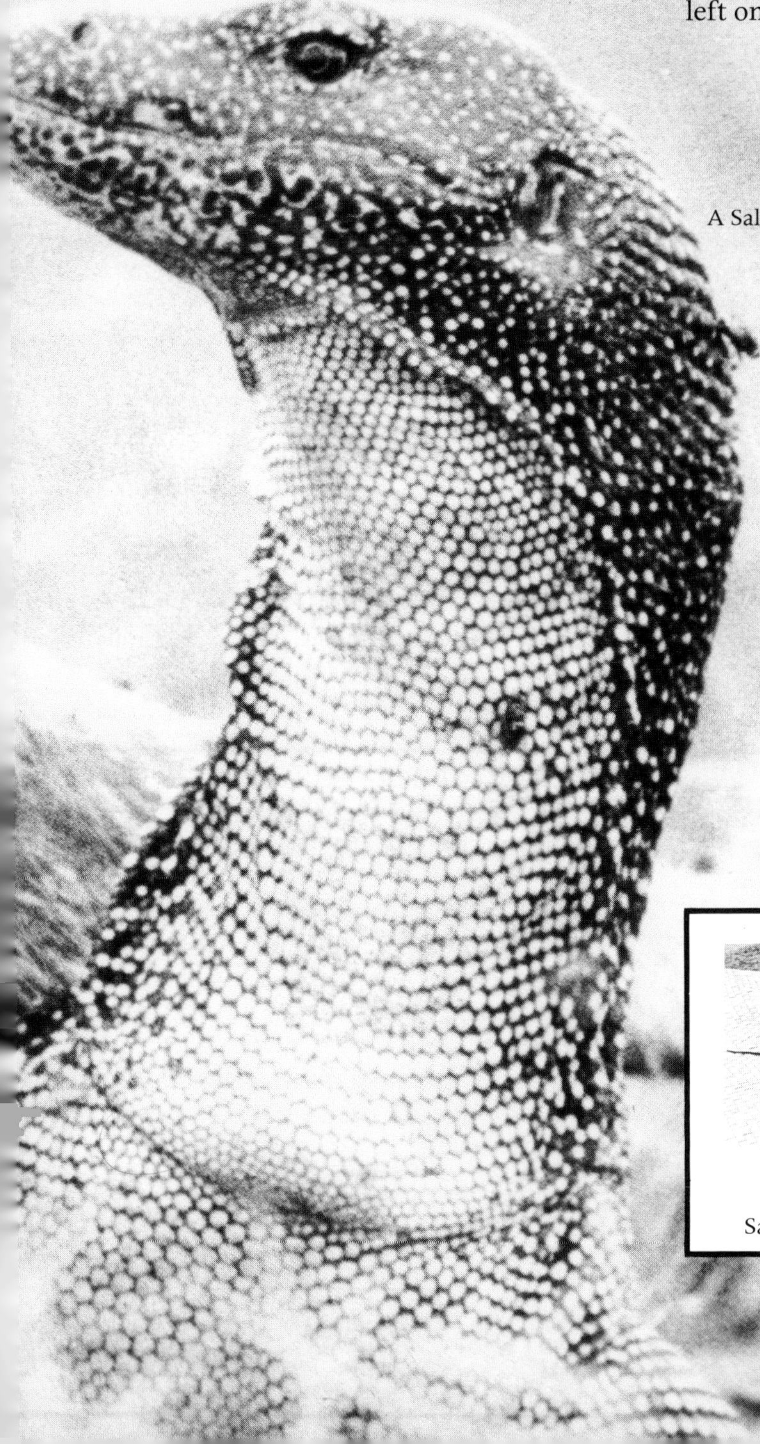

A Salvadori Dragon, discovered on Operation Drake.

This photograph shows the length of one Salvadori Dragon found on Operation Drake.

Chapter Three

Monsters Down Below

Below the thunders of the upper deep,
Far, far beneath in the abysmal sea
His ancient, dreamless, uninvaded sleep
The Kraken sleepeth.

Alfred Lord Tennyson

'There's something strange on the radar screen!' exclaimed the colonel in charge of the atomic test in the Arctic. The explosions gave him a tremendous sense of his own power – 'I feel I'm helping to write a new chapter in Genesis' – but he was unaware that he had disturbed a creature from the prehistoric past, entombed in the ice for millions of years.

Witnesses of the nuclear test glimpsed the monster, but when the reports reached New York they were dismissed by the experts: 'If all the reports of monsters were put together, they would reach the moon.'

This does not mean to say that the experts are right. You only have to think of the animals who hibernate during the winter in an apparently lifeless state without food or drink to realize that creatures can exist without any form of nourishment for a long time. There was proof of this in 1981 when a lacquered box bought by a British family on holiday at the seaside a few years earlier was dropped by accident, and one of the decorative shells was seen to move. This small creature had been glued to the box, covered with lacquer, and kept in a hot room without moisture – yet the snail survived and was even returned to the sands at Blackpool to start life all over again.

In the USA human beings have arranged for their bodies to be kept in deep-freeze in order to be revived in years to come when medical science might resurrect them. Anything is possible. If humans can be packed in ice, why can't a prehistoric monster be preserved in the Arctic?

While the doctors and experts in New York were dismissing such an idea, claiming that no animal could survive off its own tissue for a period of 100 million years, the monster was sighted swimming towards the city by the captain of a fishing-trawler.

'It's unbelievable,' he shouted into his transmitter, 'it's tremendous . . . I can only see part of it . . . but the most astonishing thing is . . .' The link was cut off and he was never heard from again, his trawler assumed to be sunk, or capsized.

Finally the monster did reach New York and was identified as a *Rhedosaurus*. It caused panic as it waded on shore. When it started to wreck a fairground scientists shot an isotope into it and it was burnt to death.

It shouldn't happen to a monster – and it didn't. The monster, though not the lacquered snail or the deep-freeze humans just mentioned, was fantasy – the beast from 20 000 fathoms from the film of the same name. A creature released from the past by a nuclear or volcanic explosion, which goes on the rampage when it reaches civilization, is a popular theme of monster movies.

The coelacanth

That was fiction, but this is fact.

Fishermen off the coast of South Africa were mystified by the strange creature sometimes landed in their nets. They described it as a 'savage, huge, lumbering monstrosity', unlike any other fish they had seen. Usually the creature was dead and they threw it back, but one that they caught was alive. They kept clear of its vicious, snapping teeth, until it died three hours later.

In 1938 a South African professor, J C B Smith, was shown one of these creatures. Though it was in a bad state of decay he was astounded by what he saw, and offered a reward for another, better specimen. It was not until 1952 that a second was fished up off the coast of Madagascar and his suspicions were confirmed – the monster was a coelacanth, one of the lungfish with teeth and a hollow spine known as *Crossopterygii* which lived 300 million years ago and which everyone believed had been extinct for the last 70 million years.

Real or fake? This 'sea monster' was photographed by Robert Le Serrec in Stonehaven Bay, Hook Island, Australia on 2 December, 1964.

Everyone believed that coelacanths were extinct until one was caught by fishermen off the coast of South Africa.

The coelacanth provided living proof that the dead are not so dead as the experts think, though few of the coelacanths caught since then, by fishermen who now appreciate their value, have lived for more than a few hours in captivity.

The rediscovery of the coelacanth has great significance: with stout pectoral fins which could have been used as flipper-like arms or legs if stranded on land, the coelacanth is a vital link back to prehistoric fish and the process of evolution. Also, if one 'extinct' species is found to be alive after 70 million years, could the legends of sea-serpents lurking in the deep be true after all? Certainly they have been consistent over the years.

In 1734, a Danish missionary to Greenland reported a strange object, since named the Kraken, swimming off the coast:

> 'The monster was of so huge a size that, coming out of the water, its head reached as high as a mainmast; its body was as bulky as the ship, and three or four times as long. It had a long pointed snout, and spouted like a whale; it had great broad paws; the body seemed covered with shellwork, and the skin was very ragged and uneven. The under part of its body was shaped like an enormous huge serpent and when it dived again under the water, it plunged backward into the sea, and so raised its tail aloft, which seemed a whole ship's length distance from the bulkiest part of its body.'

There is no reason to doubt this man's story. There may well be sea-serpents of which we are unaware, just as we thought that the coelacanth was extinct, but it is possible that the Danish missionary saw a giant squid instead. These can reach immense proportions: one of the largest ever caught, off Newfoundland in 1871, had a body 6 m (20 ft) long and one tentacle which stretched to 10 m (32 ft). Glimpsed in the water, even part of a giant squid could be mistaken for a serpent.

A fleshy red serpent once seen floating on the water by an American sea captain proved to be the arm of an octopus 13 m (45 ft) long and 75 cms (2·5 ft) thick, with large suckers.

The illustrations by Henry Lee in *Sea Monsters Unmasked* clearly show how easily a partly submerged squid could be mistaken for a sea-serpent. Depending on the angle, the thickest end of a tentacle rising from the water could resemble a tail, suggesting a vast body underneath the surface, longer and larger than the ship itself.

Whenever 'gigantic arms' are referred to, a squid might be responsible.

This illustration from *The Mysteries of the Ocean* (1870) written by Arthur Magin shows how a giant squid might have been mistaken for the legendary Kraken.

The surface of the Atlantic was once so calm that three sailors were ordered to go over the side of the ship to paint the hull, but as they were lowered by ropes on a plank a serpent appeared and stretched out an arm which seized two of the men while the third screamed for help. Other sailors raced across the deck to save him, hacking desperately at the arm until they managed to chop it off with their axes. The monster's arm was described as 7·5 m (25 ft) long and as thick as a tree-trunk, with suckers the size of saucepan lids, so it is not altogether surprising that the rescued sailor died from his shocking experience that night.

In 1942, after a troopship was sunk in the South Atlantic, a huge arm snatched one of the three survivors in a lifeboat and fastened around his leg. The other men held on to him with all their strength and saved his life, though the red suckers with a ring of teeth left their scars as proof of the incident. However, genuine mistakes explain other cases.

One American captain who thought he had found a sea-serpent pulled his haul on board deck – only to find a mass of flotsam tangled up with seaweed.

The remains of a serpent could be a dead basking shark, parts of which fall away when it rots leaving a small skull and a long vertebrae or back-bone which could be mistaken for a neck. Two sea-creatures swimming alongside each other could be seen as one immense creature: migrating whales, for example, are frequently accompanied by black sharks.

Even so, in spite of sea-monsters being confused with giant squids and other logical explanations being found for them, so many reports of sea-monsters have persisted up to the present day that it would be foolish to deny the existence of monsters of the deep – especially in view of the rediscovery of the coelacanth. These are some of the stories which defy explanation.

In 1848 the British warship *HMS Daedalus* reported the sighting of a sea-serpent swimming towards the ship. It had a mane on its back like that of a horse, and a neck which jutted out 1·2 m (4 ft) with a patch of white on it.

The crew watched it for 30 minutes and estimated it was 18 m (60 ft) long, with a smallish, snake-like brown head.

One of the most recent sightings comes from the two British soldiers and navigators, Capt John Ridgway and Sgt Chay Blyth, who rowed the Atlantic in 1966. One midnight they were baffled when they 'suddenly saw the writhing, twisting shape of a great creature. It was outlined by the phosphorescence in the sea as if a string of neon lights was hanging from it. It was an enormous size, some 10 m (35 ft) long, and it came toward (us) quite fast. I must have watched it for some ten seconds,' says Capt Ridgway. 'I reluctantly had to believe that there was only one thing it could have been – a sea-serpent.'

This model of the Ogopogo, Lake Okanagan's monster, is at Kelowna in British Columbia, Canada.

USOs – unidentified swimming objects

Serpents are not confined to the depths of the sea – there are many freshwater monsters which lurk on the bottom of lakes, if we believe the reports. The Loch Ness Monster is not alone.

One of the most popular serpents was called the Ogopogo. It was seen in the last century in Lake Okanagan in British Columbia, Canada, when an arm reached out and pulled a horse from the shore into the water. The local Indians called it the Naitaka, but the white settlers chose the nickname of Ogopogo which caught the public imagination and became famous in a music-hall song:

'His mother was an earwig,
His father was a whale;
A little bit of head,
And hardly any tail.
And Ogopogo was his name!'

An American family, the Watsons from Montreal, saw the Ogopogo in 1949. They said it had 'a long sinuous body, 9 m (30 ft) in length, consisting of about five undulations, each about 1·5 m (5 ft) long, apparently separated from each other by about a 60-cm (2-ft) space.' He added that the head was only 'a little bit' of a thing, which contrasts with the opinion of the woman who saw the Ogopogo clearly as it surfaced three times before it disappeared, but thought it looked beautiful with a head resembling that of a horse. And in 1959 the publisher of the *Vernon Advertiser* was cruising down the lake at a modest 16 km/h (10 mph) when he was overtaken by the Ogopogo which had the same five humps but a snake-like head.

At first these descriptions do not add up. You would expect a sea-serpent to have a head like a snake's, but hardly that of a horse unless it was a creature like a sea-horse. Yet a serpent with a horse's head has been reported time and time again, so it has to be taken seriously.

The most startling evidence suggests that it could be a giant snake with a very large head. This was the claim of a Dutch helicopter pilot a few years ago who spotted an immense dark green snake, with a white belly, when he was flying over Africa. When he circled closer, the snake actually rose up 3 m (10 ft) out of the water to strike the helicopter and the pilot was able to see the head, about 60 cm (2 ft) wide, like that of 'a very large horse which could easily have eaten a man.'

When the Dutch pilot circled closer, the snake rose up out of the water to strike the helicopter.

Loading scuba gear, used in the hunt for the Champ of Lake Champlain.

This makes one think again. The common characteristics of freshwater monsters are the humps – which could be the coils in the snake's body – and the horse's head. As for the horse's mane, this could be nothing more than weed waving in the water.

There is another explanation for the differing descriptions – there could be a family of such creatures, the male and female and their young having different features.

It is easy to mistake a moving object in the water. As the tide advances up an estuary a ridge of rock will look as if it is moving as parts are exposed by the rippling currents, making them look like humps. Tricks of light on water can achieve astonishing effects with an object as simple as a floating log, or three gulls in single file. However, there are so many reports of serpents with five humps and a horse's head that the Ogopogo cannot be dismissed.

The Champ of Lake Champlain

This sighting took place half an hour's drive from New York, near the borders of Canada, in Lake Champlain which has an outlet to the sea. Reports of a water-monster go back to 1609 – it is supposedly 12 m (40 ft) long and as thick as a barrel, with the familiar horse-like head.

What makes this case of particular interest is the number of local residents who claim to have seen it clearly, though the only polaroid snap is so blurred that it does not prove anything at all. This has a significant similarity with the vague photographs of the Loch Ness Monster, as we shall see.

Confirmation of the monster comes from Dr Roy Mackal who believes that it is a 'serpentine whale' supposedly extinct for 20 million years, but somehow stranded by time in this inland sea.

Meanwhile, the Mayor of Port Henry is sufficiently impressed to have issued orders forbidding anyone to shoot at the Champ should it surface again.

A Chinese water monster

This report of a water-monster comes from the same remote region of Tibet where the Yeti is supposed to live. In 1981 Chinese scientists investigated rumours of a creature which had emerged from a lake and eaten both a farmer and his cow – at least that is what the local people assumed, for the man was 'dragged down' and never seen again.

The lake where this monster is believed to live is Wenbu Lake, which covers 1240 sq km (480 sq miles), big enough to conceal an entire race of such monsters.

On another occasion, the monster was seen by three witnesses who stood at the edge of the water 'and saw on the surface a strange animal. Its body was as big as a house, like a dinosaur's, its neck was very long, and its head was comparatively small.'

Similar descriptions of different monsters are reported all over the world. These monsters seem to resemble the fish-eating *Plesiosaur* which existed millions of years ago, or its successor the *Mosaur*, a sea-lizard 12 m (40 ft) long.

With the example of the rediscovered coelacanth, who dares to say that such creatures have not survived? Inevitably, this leads us to the most celebrated monster of them all.

The creature emerged from the lake, and neither the man nor his cow were ever seen again.

The greatest monster of them all

First of all, the facts: Loch Ness is 40 km (24 miles) long, 1·5 km (1 mile) wide, and is estimated at 230 m (750 ft) deep. This is as deep as the deepest part of the North Sea. Anything could live there.

Probably Loch Ness was connected to the sea 6000 years ago – a link with the Champ and the inland sea of Lake Champlain – and there could even be an underground tunnel today providing access to the sea, explaining why the Loch Ness Monster is only seen at occasional intervals. The loch is freshwater.

There have been so many sightings of the Loch Ness Monster (commonly known as Nessie) over the years that they cannot all be dismissed as lies or hoaxes. From the 1930s onwards sightings came in rapid succession, catching the imagination of the public.

Probably the first people to sight the monster in this century were Mr and Mrs MacKay in March 1933 when they were returning from a sale in Inverness:

> 'Suddenly, at the seven-mile [11 km] stone . . . you couldn't believe what you were seeing, never having seen such an enormous thing . . . you could not put a name to it. It could have been an elephant or a whale . . .'

Mrs MacKay told this to a *Daily Mail* reporter in March 1983, breaking her silence after 50 years. 'I was yelling to John to stop but he only thought a bee was bothering me on the windscreen.' By the time her husband did stop the car, all he could see were the ripples but he knew something big had been there a moment before. Mr MacKay told his wife not to mention this to anyone, in case people thought they had been drinking, but she did tell someone in 'strictest confidence' who told the water bailiff, Alex Campbell, who told Dr Evan Barron, the editor of the *Courier* newspaper.

On the afternoon of July 22, 1933, Mr and Mrs George Spicer were driving along the south bank of the loch on their way home to London, when a vast creature emerged from the bracken on the hill. They watched with amazement and horror as it lumbered across the road with a small animal (probably a lamb) in its mouth, then splashed into the water. Though the incident only lasted for a few seconds, they were able to describe the monster vividly as 'a loathsome sight', like a gigantic snail with a long neck and a tiny head on a bulky body. It moved on flippers and was elephant-grey in colour.

In 1934 the monster was seen for the first time by the water bailiff Alex Campbell. He has seen the monster eighteen times since then, and is now retired and in his eighties.

In 1934 the most famous photograph was taken of the monster, as it rose out of the loch with its long neck above the surface. The photograph was taken by Mr R K Wilson with a quarter-plate camera, but cannot be regarded as proof.

During the next 40 years an astonishing 3000 sightings were reported. Many of these were genuine mistakes, and the Director of the London Aquarium dismissed them altogether as 'a striking example of mass hallucination'.

There was a practical reason for sighting the monster – money. Rewards for the capture of Nessie ranged from five hundred dollars offered by the New York Zoo; twenty thousand pounds from Bertram Mills' Circus in Britain; rising to a million pounds from a whisky manufacturer. Public interest became so keen that a Member of Parliament demanded an official investigation into the 'monster matter' but was told by the government that it was 'more properly a matter for the private enterprise of scientists aided by the zeal of press and photographers.' Sure enough the investigations into the existence of the monster did become more serious and scientific.

In 1962 David James, a Member of Parliament at the time, and also a Highland laird who had founded the Loch Ness Phenomena Investigation Bureau, kept watch on the loch. He saw an object in pursuit of a salmon, and reached this conclusion.

'We find that there is some unidentified, animate object in Loch Ness which, if it be mammal, reptile, fish or mollusc of any known order, is of such a size as to be worthy of careful scientific examination and identification. If it is not of a known order, it represents a challenge which is only capable of being answered by controlled investigation on carefully scientific principles.'

Dr Rines' diving team took flash-lit photographs of an object which they claimed was the monster.

Alex Campbell (left), and Dr Evan Barron (right), with the 1934 photo of the monster.

Taking advantage of the latest diving equipment, a distinguished team led by Dr Robert Rines, President of Boston's Academy of Applied Science, penetrated the deep, dark water of the loch in 1975. They took flash-lit photographs of an object which they claimed was the monster, indicating a large body with a neck approximately 3 m (10 ft) long. The wildlife artist and authority, Sir Peter Scott, son of the famous explorer, gave the team his support: 'The new evidence, taken with the old, suggests that there are indeed large animals in Loch Ness . . . This is, for me, the only possible conclusion.' The team believed it was a *Plesiosaur* – the marine reptile thought to be extinct – and Scott christened it with a special name, *Nessitera Rhombopteryx*, meaning 'Ness Monster with the Diamond Fin'.

It is a clumsy nickname and someone wrote a letter to *The Times*, London, pointing out that it is an anagram of *Monster hoax by Sir Peter*. This created considerable laughter and controversy; however, Scott has assured the author of this book that his belief was genuine. Confirming his statement, he announced, 'I would stake all my knowledge of human relations on the fact that this is no hoax perpetrated by the people who took the pictures.' Even so, the coincidence of the anagram raised doubts.

Further experiments were going to include dolphins carrying sonar equipment and cameras, but as they are saltwater animals they would have suffered extreme stress in the freshwater loch and the idea was abandoned.

In the summer of 1980, a further expedition started investigations, led by Adrian Shine of the Loch Ness and Morar Project. Using a 12-m (40-ft) raft, he towed a special dredging device 'based on the idea that if there are live monsters in the lake there must also be dead ones. If we bring to the surface any bones of ancient creatures we shall have gone a long way to establishing the reality of Loch Ness monsters.' However, no bones were discovered.

Dr Robert Rines (right) at Loch Ness with an underwater camera during the mid-1970s search for the monster.

The absence of bones is one of the baffling aspects of the case of the Loch Ness Monster. If the creature belongs to a previous age, it is reasonable to assume there have been generations of such creatures to ensure survival. The idea of a single monster lasting for millions of years is impossible, unless it were recently disturbed, like the beast from 20 000 fathoms. But if there have been families of monsters, why have no bones been found when boats and even a Wellington bomber which crashed in 1940 have been discovered on the bottom 67 m (220 ft) down, in a good state of preservation?

The underground tunnel could be one explanation. However, the density of the mud at the bottom of the loch is a more convincing theory. This is so deep that bones could sink out of reach, especially if the monster followed the curious habit of the crocodile which swallows a stone when it is dying in order to fall to the bottom of the lake or river where it lives.

There is no doubt that the mud on the bottom of Loch Ness is exceptionally deep and the water unusually dense. This is because of the peat washed down by the dozens of mountain streams which join the five rivers that pour into the loch.

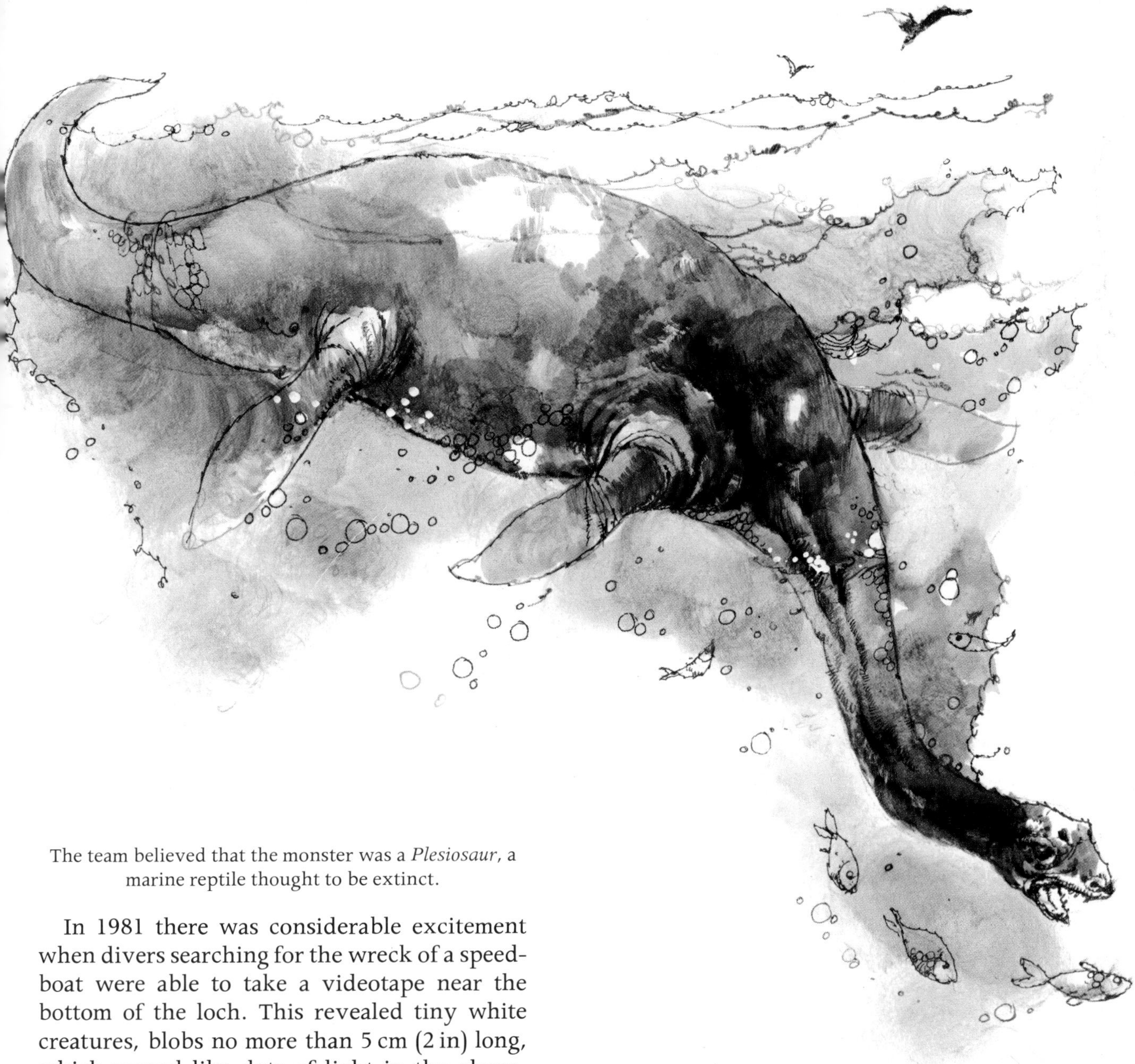

The team believed that the monster was a *Plesiosaur*, a marine reptile thought to be extinct.

In 1981 there was considerable excitement when divers searching for the wreck of a speedboat were able to take a videotape near the bottom of the loch. This revealed tiny white creatures, blobs no more than 5 cm (2 in) long, which moved like dots of light in the gloom. Because these dots could not be identified, it was argued that if an unknown species of crustaceans or insects existed at such depths, there could be a species of monster too.

Such claims are interesting but they are not evidence. Indeed, in view of the thousands of so-called sightings, it is strange that no irrefutable evidence has been produced. Photographs are vague and blurred, and the Loch Ness Monster has shown extraordinary skill in vanishing whenever people try to catch it, sometimes by a mere matter of seconds due to faulty equipment. Does the lack of proof suggest a pattern? Is it no coincidence but a part of the phenomenon? Is the absence of evidence, evidence in itself?

This becomes a detective puzzle in which the absence of clues are evidence, like Sherlock Holmes and 'the curious incident of the dog in the night-time'.

'"The dog did nothing in the night-time," protested Dr Watson.

"That was the curious incident," remarked Sherlock Holmes.'

If Holmes had been called in to investigate the Loch Ness Monster, he might have come to a similar conclusion about the curious evidence concerning the monster.

There is no factual evidence.

Exactly, that is what makes the case so curious!

Narrow escapes

Nessie's vanishing trick is nothing new. Other monsters in other lakes have enjoyed similar narrow escapes, such as the 'water-cow' seen by the novelist Sir Walter Scott in a loch near his home in 1827. With his friends, he used a form of 'nightbait' to try to drag the creature on to dry land. A dog was killed for the purpose, fastened to a small anchor and hung from a boat. It sounds clumsy, but when they returned in the morning and pulled the bait on shore they were surprised to find it had not been touched.

The Wyvern Monster lived in the Welsh lake of Cynwich several centuries ago. Its story was translated from an ancient scroll by Stephen Jones and published in 1921. The Wyvern Monster had several humps. During the day it basked in the sun by the edge of the lake, uncoiled and relaxed as it gazed lazily into the water. At night it was transformed, moving stealthily inland in search of food and leaving a slimy trail.

A local chieftain offered a reward if archers killed it, but their failure is significant: 'It was never possible to catch even a glimpse of the Wyvern on the days when the bowmen were waiting. It was as though some subtle knowledge came to its brain and bade it beware.'

Loch Ness is in Invernesshire in Scotland. Its calm exterior gives no clues about what might lurk beneath.

The similarity to the Loch Ness Monster is obvious, and one of the 'monster-hunters' and experts on the subject, F W Holiday, who wrote *The Dragon and the Disc* (1973), has commented that the ancient scroll might have been written today – 'with regard to the abnormal difficulty of filming the Loch Ness Monster. This being so, it looks very much as if the Wyvern legend was based on actual observations.'

Nessie is certainly camera-shy. In 1965 the Loch Ness Investigation Bureau maintained a watch for six months with cameras at the ready, yet they had no luck, although the monster was seen by numerous witnesses without cameras during that same period.

Is this underwater photograph proof that the Loch Ness monster exists? It was taken in June 1975 by Dr Robert Rines and his team.

In the summer of 1970 another observer-photographer kept watch at Strone Point overlooking Urquhart Castle. Finally he became so fed up that he abandoned his watch at six in the evening, packing up his equipment. Within moments, the monster was seen by Fred Anderson, his wife and two children who had stopped to admire the view. They watched the object moving around the castle until it headed into the loch and disappeared. If the Strone camera had been manned, the whole scene could have been recorded – or could it? Avoiding the camera suggests a radar-like cunning on the part of the animal which is beyond credibility. Holiday reached the final conclusion that:

> 'Normal animals do not behave in such an inexplicable way (always frustrating detection) because they cannot; therefore you had to conclude that the peculiarities were due to chance. This was the prevailing attitude amongst investigators. An explanation based on chance seemed to me most unsatisfactory. Chance is a random effect; it is just as likely to work in favour of the investigator as against him. If the ten years of intensive effort at Loch Ness which resulted in failure to get a detailed film was the result of chance, then it was not a random effect and the expression became meaningless. In that event, the explanation lay elsewhere.'

Holiday reached the fantastic conclusion that the Loch Ness Monster does not exist as solid matter at all, and compared the elusiveness of USOs (unidentified swimming objects) to the space equivalent, the UFOs, listing their points in common. USOs and UFOs both: change shape and vary in colour; produce wild excitement in domestic animals such as dogs; move at great speed; and never leave excreta or other traces (such as bones). Their apparitions are usually partly hidden or indistinct, and no one has captured either of them.

The Andersons watched the object moving around the castle until it headed into the loch and disappeared.

In 1967 an electronics engineer called Dick Raynor, a monster hunter for many years, filmed a moving object in Loch Ness, but he reached this significant conclusion: 'Something about the monster is not quite real. I'm not sure you would feel anything if you touched it.'

Colin Wilson, a foremost authority on the occult, examined this explanation in his book *Mysteries* (1976). 'When he [Holiday] also noticed the frequency of UFO sightings above lakes where there are reports of monsters, he came to the conclusion that he was not dealing with real dragons or discs, but with some archetypal symbol of good and evil.'

This theory has been taken even further by a teacher called Jenny Randles, the director of investigations for the British UFO Research Association, who gives this explanation: 'Loch Ness stands on a fault – or ley – line in the earth which runs across north Scotland. This, combined with a large body of water, means a super-intense electro-magnetic field is developed. This is strong enough to cause black-outs among people who then imagine something strange has happened.' She claims that UFO sightings occur, 'when rocks under stress generate electrical energy which is passed through water, creating light or balls of fire in the sky. These are not flying saucers any more than Nessie is an actual monster.'

In other words, the Loch Ness Monster is an illusion, caused by natural phenomena. This is a highly convincing theory but it does not explain why we should see something in the shape of a prehistoric animal, unless we accept Holiday's theory that it is a symbol of evil, like the dragon slain by St George. However, so many honest people have seen the Loch Ness Monster this century – more than 3000 sightings altogether – that I believe there is a further solution.

The Loch Ness mystery solved?

The monster may be a visual echo from the past – a ghost. You may laugh at this suggestion, but if you believe there are such things as ghosts – as most people do – consider this carefully.

A ghost is an impression left on the atmosphere, like a negative on a camera-plate, which can be seen years later by a sensitive person in the right atmosphere and conditions. Frequently, the impression is left when something violent has happened – like a murder or suicide. Battlefield hauntings, where figures are seen and heard at a place of former bloodshed, are particularly common. If there had been a prehistoric monster, like a *Plesiosaur*, in or around Loch Ness millions of years ago, it is conceivable that today we see the impression of this creature.

This would explain the absence of bones; the failure to capture the monster on film, for it is impossible to photograph a ghost even though many people have tried; and the apparent contradictions of other monster sightings, like the one seen by three reliable witnesses in Lough Fadda, an Irish lake in Connemara. This lake is far too small to hold such a monster today. It would have eaten all the fish and soon have died from lack of food.

There is one suggested link with the past, made by Colin Wilson, who has pointed out that: 'All kinds of strange phenomena have been observed over leys – particularly at the nodal points: ghosts, ghouls and poltergeists . . .'

If you believe in the ghosts of dead human beings, or their dogs, why not accept the ghosts of monsters? Nessie could simply be a freak of visual telepathy with the prehistoric past, when such monsters were an everyday reality.

It is understandable that many people cannot accept the possibility of such a ghostly explanation. If so, they will take a special interest in the new scientific investigation which promises to come up with hard fact after a search which has lasted for ten years. The leader, Adrian Shine, claims that sophisticated equipment produced a sonar trace in 1982 which was tracked for 68 seconds and 'seemed to dive from 230 to 375 ft [70 to 115 m] at a speed of 5 mph [8 km/h].' This is a great depth, but Adrian Shine has reached this conclusion: 'If there are large creatures in Loch Ness, then they would appear on sonar just as we have recorded them.'

This impressed the British bookmakers to such an extent that William Hill dropped the odds from 50-1 to 25-1 in the same year on the chances of finding the Monster in Loch Ness. But we are still waiting for 'evidence'.

This realistic Loch Ness monster is in fact a model.

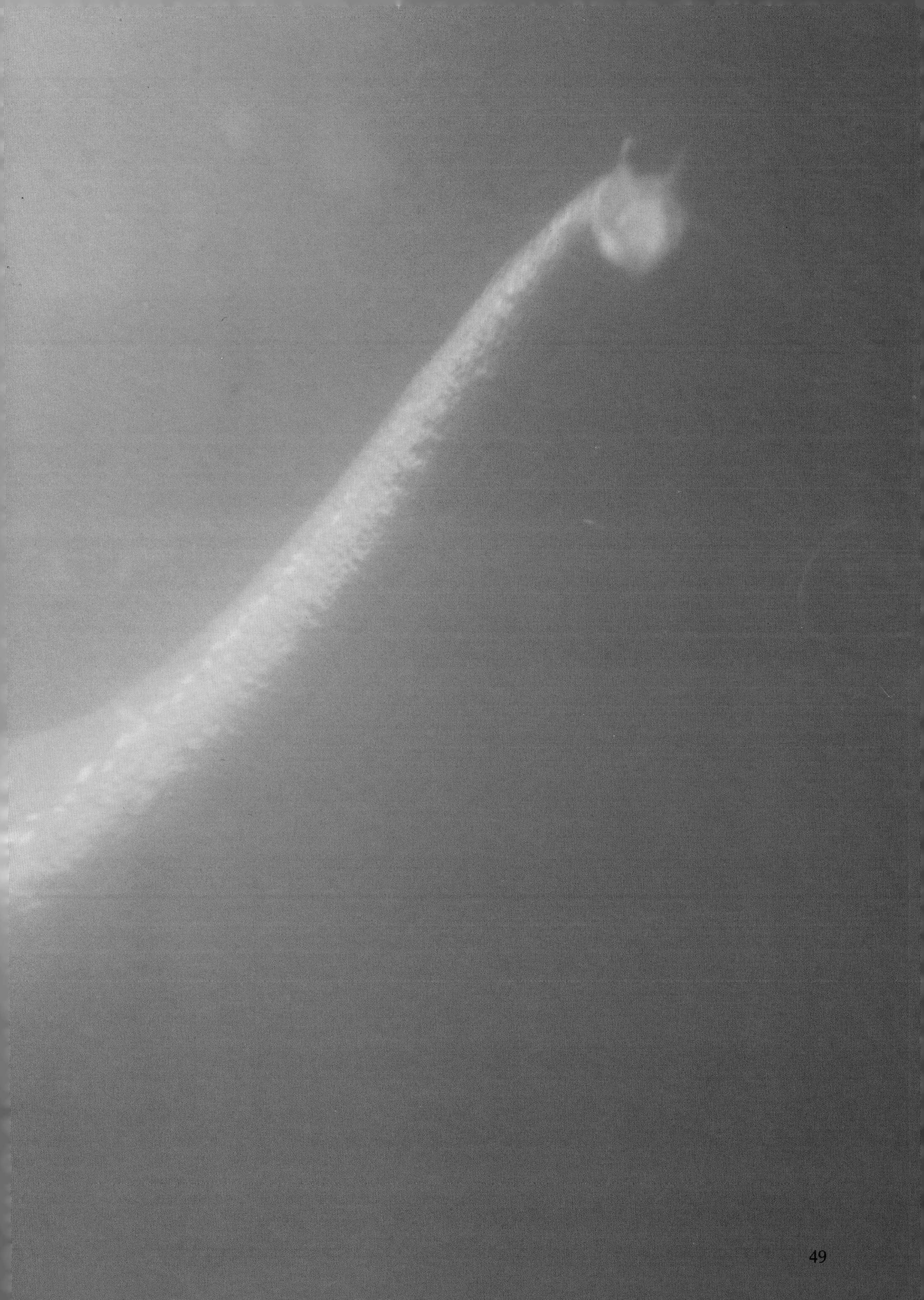

Chapter Four

Strange Stories of Monstrous Creatures

The worm's hole appeared to breathe forth death in its most repulsive form.

Bram Stoker

The beasts in Greek and Roman mythology have a symbolic importance, like the dragon, as examples of evil. Heads of the monster called Medusa were used to decorate the tomb-like coffins in Greece two thousand years ago. These heads are fierce and open-mouthed, to warn robbers that they would be turned to stone if they dared to break open the coffins in search of loot. Medusa was one of the three ferocious Gorgons who had snakes entwined in their hair.

Medusa and the Gorgons

The three Gorgons began as three beautiful girls called Stheino, Euryale and Medusa. Later they became sea monsters.

Medusa fell in love with Poseidon, the God of the Sea. This displeased Athena, the Olympian goddess of wisdom, ruler of storms, and the guardian of Athens where the Parthenon was built as her temple. Athena took a cruel revenge, changing Medusa into a hideous monster with snakes for hair, teeth like tusks, glaring eyes and claws. Her expression could turn a man into stone if he dared to look at her, which is why Medusa heads were put on the tombs to frighten away thieves.

When Perseus, the son of Zeus and Danae, learned that King Polydectes was scheming to marry his mother, he offered him any gift he cared to name – even the Gorgon Medusa's head – if he promised to give up his plan.

King Polydectes accepted gleefully, expecting Perseus to be killed in such a dangerous test of courage, but Perseus had friends to help him. Hermes gave him a sickle with the sharpness of a diamond. He still needed winged sandals so he could fly; a magic satchel to hold the severed head; and the dark helmet of invisibility which once belonged to Hades. All these objects were in the possession of Medusa's sisters, the other two Gorgons who were even uglier than she was with a single eye between them. Perseus managed to steal this eye, demanding the magic weapons in exchange for returning it.

The Gorgons surrendered them and Perseus flew on his winged sandals to a sinister landscape strewn with the stone shapes of men who had been petrified by Medusa's gaze.

Taking care only to see her reflection in his shield and not with his naked eye, which would have turned him into stone like the others, he cut off her hideous head with a single stroke of the razor-sharp sickle. The drops of blood that fell into the sea on his journey back became the scarlet branches of coral which form a sea-fan known to this day as gorgonia, while the name gorgon has entered our language as 'a terrible or repulsive woman'.

Perseus flew back with Medusa's head in the magic satchel, but this victorious triumph was not the end of the story. When Perseus entered the court with his prize, he found that King Polydectes was celebrating his marriage to his mother, Danae, having intended to break his word all along.

Angered by such deceit, Perseus slowly removed Medusa's head from the magic satchel, careful to turn his head away so he should not gaze on it himself, and as he twisted the gruesome features towards the king and his courtiers he turned the whole assembly to stone. Rescuing his mother, Perseus left the court with his wife, Andromeda, and they travelled to Argos where he had been born. An oracle had warned his grandfather, Acrisius, that Perseus would cause his death, so when his grandson arrived Acrisius left quickly for another country. Unluckily, or by the will of the gods, Perseus was invited there to take part in a discus contest. When he threw his disc it was blown off course, killing his grandfather and fulfilling the prophecy. In his grief, so the legend claims, Perseus travelled to Asia where his son Perses became king, giving his name to the Persian race.

Medusa and the two ferocious Gorgons had snakes entwined in their hair. One look from Medusa could turn people into stone.

Odysseus and the Cyclops

The Cyclopes were also monsters with a single eye, though they had one each – in the centre of the forehead. In Homer's long poem called *The Odyssey*, written in the 10th century BC, the traveller and hero Odysseus describes how he came to the land of the Cyclopes. These were fierce, uncivilized giants who never lifted a hand to plant or plough but plundered anything which lived, such as the wild, roaming goats which they killed for food. 'The Cyclopes have no assemblies for making laws, nor any settled customs, but live in hollow caverns in the mountain heights, where each man is a lawgiver to his children and his wives, and nobody cares a jot for his neighbours.'

Odysseus vowed to kill their leader Polyphemus, who quickly captured him instead.

> 'The cruel brute jumped up, and reaching out towards my men, seized a couple and dashed their heads against the floor as though they had been puppies. Their brains ran out on the ground and soaked the earth. Limb by limb he tore them to pieces to make his meal, which he devoured like a mountain lion, never pausing till entrails and flesh, marrow and bones, were all consumed, while we could do nothing but weep and lift up our hands to Zeus in horror at the ghastly sight, paralysed by our utter sense of hopelessness. When the Cyclopes had filled his great belly with this meal of human flesh, which he washed down with unwatered milk, he stretched himself out to sleep among his flocks inside the cave.'

Odysseus felt for his scabbard, intending to kill the monster, when he remembered he and his men were sealed in by a huge rock which the Cyclops had pushed into the mouth of the cave. They were trapped – so Odysseus started to sharpen a long branch of young olive-wood instead, cutting it into a point.

The next day, pretending to accept defeat, Odysseus greeted the Cyclops with a bowl of wine and flattered him: 'I brought it for you by way of an offering in the hope that you would be charitable and help me on my homeward way. But your savagery is more than we can bear. Cruel monster, how can you expect ever to have a visitor again from the world of men, after such deeds as you have done?'

Lulled by the wine and the submissive words, the Cyclops continued to drink from the bowl. Three times Odysseus filled it up for him, and three times the monster drained the bowl to the dregs. At last, when the wine had befuddled his wits, Odysseus addressed the Cyclops suavely. 'Cyclops,' he said, 'you wish to know the name I bear . . . My name is Nobody.'

Odysseus had hardly spoken this curious name when the Cyclops collapsed from the wine, falling face upwards on the floor, where he lay with his great neck twisted to one side, asleep.

Now Odysseus took his revenge. Seizing the olive pole, his men used it to blind the Cyclops. The wretched monster gave a howl of pain as this took place, so deafening that it brought the other Cyclopes running to the outside of the cave. 'What has happened?' they shouted, listening to his fearful screams.

Odysseus' cleverness and cunning were now revealed, for the Cyclops cried back in reply, 'O my friends, it's Nobody's treachery that is doing me to death.' The other Cyclopes shook their heads outside but offered little sympathy. 'Well then,' they answered, 'if *nobody* is assaulting you in your solitude, you must be sick. Sickness comes from almighty Zeus and cannot be helped. All you can do is pray to your father, the Lord Poseidon.'

And they went away! How could they pity or help their leader if nobody had attacked him!

Odysseus had worked out how to escape from the cave. At daybreak, Odysseus and his men clung to the under-belly of the goats as Cyclops felt his way to the mouth of the cave and unblocked it in order to let the animals go out to graze. As the goats passed him his great hands searched their backs, but because he was now blind he could not see the men underneath as they made their escape.

Once they were free, Odysseus yelled back that his name was not Nobody after all.

'Cyclops,' he called to the wounded monster, 'if anyone ever asks how you came by your blindness, tell him your eye was put out by Odysseus!'

Lulled by the wine and the submissive words, the Cyclops continued to drink from the bowl.

One of Odysseus' companions escaping from the Cyclops, Polyphemus.

The Three Furies

Although these ancient monsters seem grotesque to us now, in their time they symbolized political and religious beliefs. The Three Furies, for example, have been interpreted as pangs of conscience. Also known as the *Erinyes*, they were the three daughters of Mother Earth and Air, who punished criminals by pursuing them all over the world. In spite of their useful function as early international policewomen, they looked so monstrous that people called them the 'kindly ones' (Eumenides) in order to flatter them and disguise the hideous reality of their dogs' heads and black bodies, snakes for hair, and blood-shot eyes – though at least they had two eyes each.

Far from being kindly, the furies carried whips with brass studs to make certain their victims died in agony, so a better name for them would be the three sisters of revenge.

A description by Euripides (a Greek poet who lived from about 480 to 406 BC) of one of the monsters confirms the hideousness of their looks:

'A she-dragon of hell, and all her head
Agape with fanged asps to bite me dead
She hath no face but somewhere from her cloak
Bloweth a wind of fire and bloody smoke.'

(an asp is a small venomous snake)

The head with six dogs

Envy is a constant feature of Greek mythology, resulting in terrible revenge. When Glaucus, a grandson of Bellerophon, fell in love with a beautiful water-nymph called Scylla, he appealed to Circe for help when he was rejected. Unfortunately, Circe fell in love with Glaucus. She was so jealous of her rival that she poisoned the water where Scylla swam with the juice of deadly herbs. The water-nymph was transformed into a monstrous combination of a girl's face with the heads of six wild dogs, which grabbed at passing seamen and devoured them.

Living on a rock on the Italian side of the Strait of Messina, between Italy and Sicily, Scylla was a danger to every passing ship. However, when Odysseus had to sail this way, he preferred to sail by her rather than the raging whirlpool of Charybdis on the other side, and though he sailed so close that six of his sailors were lost to the snapping heads – one for each of them – he brought his ship safely through the Strait.

Odysseus' next challenge came from the Sirens, three sea nymphs perched on rocks whose singing was so irresistible that sailors were lured too close to the rocks and wrecked their ships. The Argonaut heroes, Hercules, Bellerophon and Theseus, who slew so many ancient monsters, were saved by listening to the music of Orpheus instead. Odysseus had another plan to beat the Sirens, suggested to him by Circe. He ordered his men to plug their ears with wax as they sailed towards the rocks while he was tied to the mast. As they approached, Odysseus heard the beautiful singing of the Sirens and pleaded with his men to steer for the rocks, but they were deafened by the wax in their ears and rowed on, ignoring his orders and the song of the Sirens.

Watching Odysseus pass by to safety, the Sirens realized they were beaten and threw themselves into the water where they drowned.

The water-nymph was changed into a monstrous combination of a girl's face with the heads of six wild dogs.

This ancient Greek carving of the sea-goddess Scylla is made out of bronze.

The legend of the Lambton Worm

The English have included St George in their mythology, adopting him as a patron saint with his red cross as part of the Union Jack flag, even though the celebrated dragon-slayer achieved his conquest in North Africa.

If the Lambton Worm had been known as the Lambton Dragon, the story might be as famous in English mythology today as that of St George and the dragon – but worms sound less romantic. Also, they are real. Dragons can be fantastic in our imagination, but worms are small creepie-crawlies which we see in the garden.

The idea of a giant worm becomes more interesting when we learn that the Great Worm was a pagan symbol of evil, which is why worm legends were so prevalent in the past.

The legend goes that the Worm of Lambton lived in the River Wear near Durham in the north of England, and lurked there unnoticed until it was pulled on to the land by John de Lambton in 1420 when he decided to go fishing one Sunday morning instead of attending church – a fatal decision for which he was punished.

Instead of a fish, he landed the immense worm with nine holes on each side of its mouth, and as he pulled the large slimy monster on to the river bank he was revolted by its ugliness. Possibly because he felt guilty at missing the church service, he assumed this worm was 'the devil himself' and threw it into a deep well before going home to Sunday lunch. However, he was sadly mistaken if he thought that was the end of the story.

A few weeks later the worm returned in an angrier mood, wrapping its sinuous body around a rock in the middle of the river where it stayed all day. At night it slithered on to the land, terrorizing the neighbourhood with its attacks on cattle, swallowing whole lambs and draining cows of their milk. The unfortunate animals were said to be frozen motionless, hypnotized by the worm's 'goggly eyes', and they did not even try to escape.

Lambton became appalled by the monster he had disturbed, and tried to pay for his mistake by joining the Crusades abroad. When he returned seven years later his father told him that the worm was now more violent than ever, killing anyone who dared to go near it, uprooting trees, and demanding a tribute of milk to be left every day in barrels outside Lambton Hall. Something had to be done, and John de Lambton promised to destroy the evil worm himself. He sought the advice of the Wise Woman of Brugeford.

'You will succeed, but remember this,' she warned him. 'You must vow to kill the first living being or person you meet as you recross the threshold of Lambton Hall. If you fail, then none of the Lambtons will die in their beds for the next nine generations.'

Encouraged by her prediction of success, John de Lambton set out in a special suit of armour studded with sharp blades and spikes which would pierce the worm if it tried to coil itself around him. A terrific struggle took place, and as Lambton expected the worm did wrap itself around his body. It was so badly cut by the blades that he was able to kill it. As he waded ashore, triumphant but exhausted, he blew three blasts on his bugle. This signal was supposed to summon his loyal hound, Boris, who would then be the first living thing to meet John and would be killed – a shabby reward for the dog's faithfulness.

However, the plan misfired, for Lambton's father was so excited that he ran from the Hall and tried to embrace his son. John did not have the heart to kill his father but killed the innocent dog instead, a gesture which proved in vain.

The curse on the Lambtons began and subsequent generations died away from home, including John de Lambton who was killed on a further Crusade. Henry Lambton, the ninth lord, and Member of Parliament for Durham, was killed in June 1761 when his coach was in an accident and plunged into the River Wear, and bad luck has dogged the Lambtons up to the present day.

The worm wrapped itself around John de Lambton's body and was cut by the spikes on his armour.

This is an illustration from an 1875 book on the Lambton Worm.

The worm at Wormingford

This worm lived in the River Stour, which divides Essex and Suffolk, and was documented in 1405 as part of local folklore (translated from the medieval English by FW Holiday):

> 'Close to the town of Bures, near Sudbury, there has lately appeared, to the great hurt of the countryside, a dragon, vast in body with a crested head, teeth like a saw, and a tail extending to enormous length. Having slain the shepherd of a flock he then devoured very many sheep. There came forth in order to shoot at him with arrows the workmen of the lord on whose domain he had concealed himself, being Sir Richard de Waldegrave, knight; but the dragon's body, although struck by the archers, remained unhurt, for the arrows bounced off its back as if it were iron or hard rock. Those arrows that fell upon the spine of his back gave out as they struck a ringing or tinkling sound, just as if they had hit a brazen plate and then flew far away by reason of the hide of this great beast being impenetrable. Thereupon, in order to destroy him, all the country people around were summoned. But when the dragon saw that he was again to be assailed by arrows, he fled into a marsh or mere and there hid himself among the long reeds; nor was he any more seen.'

A mythical monster – or could there have been such a creature? It can hardly be coincidence that the village where the worm disappeared is called Wormingford, and a dragon-like worm is pictured in Wormingford Church.

St Andrew's church at Wormingford in Essex.

The worm of Spindleston Heugh

This tale involves a curse and a princess, in the best traditions. The village is near the town of Bamburgh on the coast of Northumberland. In the castle there a princess once had an argument with her wicked step-mother, who was a witch and cast this spell: 'A laidly (loathsome) worm you shall be, crawling among the rocks; a laidly worm you shall stay till your brother Wynd returns home.'

Instead of killing the worm, brave Wynd kissed its revolting head.

The curse was effective: after a storm, a hideous, writhing thing was found on the beach, before it made its home in one of the caves below the castle. At last, the brother returned to the castle and the worm emerged from its hiding-place, 'writhing and squirming along the sands after him.' Fortunately, Wynd was a young man of exceptional nerve for instead of killing the worm he kissed its revolting head. Probably a rumour had reached him of his sister's fate. Sure enough, the princess regained her normal shape and her beauty, and the wicked step-mother became a toad.

Again this story shows a battle between good and evil, but this particular legend may have been based on true events vouched for by the Laird of Mow who described a period of two years when the sea yielded no fish whatsoever though it made an unusual roaring noise. One high spring tide 'a terrible beast was cast ashore dead of the size of a man. No man could imagine anything more terrible, with horns on its head, red eyes in a shapeless face, with webbed hands and feet, and a great rump or tail hanging down to the ground; it was wasted and stank so that in a short time no man or beast could come near it . . . all the countryside saw it and many conceived great fear and terror at its appearance a long time after; it was called a sea devil.' Though the description fits that of a decomposed carcass which had been in the sea for a long time, and started to stink once on land, the instinctive reaction was to blame the devil.

The lair of the white worm

The following words were written by Bram Stoker, the author of *Dracula*, in 1911:

'In the dawn of language, the word "worm" had a somewhat different meaning from that in use today. It was an adaptation of the Anglo-Saxon "wyrm", meaning a dragon or snake; or from the Gothic "waurms", a serpent; or the Icelandic "ormur", or the German "wurm". We gather that it conveyed originally an idea of size and power, not as now in the diminutive of both these meanings. Here legendary history helps us. We have the well-known legend of the "Worm Well" of Lambton Castle, and that of the "Laidly worm of Spindleston Heugh" near Bamburgh. In both these legends the "worm" was a monster of vast size and power – a veritable dragon or serpent, such as legend attributes to vast fens or quags where there was illimitable room for expansion. A glance at a geological map will show that whatever truth there may have been of the actuality of such monsters in the early geologic periods, at least there was plenty of possibility. In England there were originally vast plains where the plentiful supply of water could gather. The streams were deep and slow, and there were holes of abysmal depth, where any kind and size of antediluvian monster could find a habitat.

'In places, which now we can see from our windows, were mudholes 100 ft (30 m) or more deep. Who can tell us when the age of the monsters which flourished in slime came to an end? There must have been places and conditions which made for greater longevity, greater size, greater strength than was usual. Such overlappings may have come down even to our earlier centuries. Nay, are there not now creatures of a vastness of bulk regarded by the generality of men as impossible? Even in our own day there are seen the traces of animals, if not the animals themselves, of stupendous size – veritable survivals from earlier ages, preserved by some special qualities in their habitats.

'Just imagine such a monster anywhere in this country, and at once we could get a sort of idea of the "worms" which possibly did frequent the great morasses which spread round the mouths of many of the great European rivers. The lair of such a monster would not have been disturbed for hundreds – or thousands – of years. Moreover, these creatures must have occupied places quite inaccessible to man. A snake which could make himself comfortable in a quagmire, 100 ft (30 m) deep, would be protected on the outskirts by such stupendous morasses as now no longer exist, or which, if they exist anywhere at all, can be in very few places on the earth's surface. Far be it from me to say that in more elemental times such things could not have been.' *The Lair of the White Worm* (1911)

Stoker was prepared to believe, and this belief was echoed by Hamilton Deane in his stage production of *Dracula* which toured Britain from 1924 with himself as the vampire-hunter Van Helsing. When the play was over, Hamilton Deane stepped before the curtain and addressed the audience: 'When you get home tonight, and the lights have been turned out, and you are afraid to look behind the curtains, and you dread to see a face appear at the window, why, just pull yourself together and remember that after all – there are such things!'

It was part of Stoker's genius that he was prepared to believe in such things as vampires, mummies, and Egyptian curses. But what Stoker did for vampires, making Dracula a household name, he failed to do for worms in his final, weird novel *The Lair of the White Worm* from which the extracts on the previous page were taken.

This book tells the story of one of the most monstrous women in fiction: Lady Arabella March. Stoker probably took this name from a Welsh family and a Welsh lake called Marchlyn Fawr, which was said to contain monsters with heads like horses. But Lady Arabella was a worm – a gigantic worm living in the depths of a well-like worm-hole.

'Look out – look out! Thc animal is furious and means to attack.'

On earth, rather than under it, Lady Arabella was transformed into a woman of curious beauty. Her new neighbour, Adam Salton, a rich young Australian who had returned to his ancestral home in the Peak District, noticed something odd about her on their first meeting when his carriage had broken down. Several black snakes were slithering on the ground and he warned her as she slipped from her own carriage with a quick gliding motion. 'She was already among the snakes when he called out . . . there seemed to be no need of warning. The snakes had turned and were wriggling back to the mound as quickly as they could. He laughed to himself behind his teeth as he whispered, "No need to fear there. They seem much more afraid of her than she of them."'

His suspicions grew the more he saw of her, especially when he was walking with a favourite mongoose perched on his shoulder – mongooses are proverbial enemies of snakes:

> 'Hitherto the mongoose had been quiet, like a playful affectionate kitten; but when the two got close, Adam was horrified to see the mongoose, in a state of the wildest fury, with every hair standing on end, jump from his shoulder and run towards Lady Arabella . . . He called a warning "Look out – look out! The animal is furious and means to attack."
>
> 'Lady Arabella looked more than ever disdainful and was passing on; the mongoose jumped at her in a furious attack. Adam rushed forward with his stick, the only weapon he had. But just as he got within striking distance, the lady drew out a revolver and shot the animal, breaking his backbone. Not satisfied with this, she poured shot after shot into him till the magazine was exhausted. There was no coolness or hauteur about her now; she seemed more furious even than the animal, her face transformed with hate, and as determined to kill as he had been. Adam, not knowing exactly what to do, lifted his hat in apology and hurried on . . .'

Lady Arabella had recognized her enemy; and it was not long before Adam Salton had to face the hideous reality, that she was a monster.

Lady Arabella impressed her other neighbours as a smart woman with a close-fitting cap of dazzling white fur and emeralds coiled around her neck, except that, 'Her voice was peculiar, very low and sweet, and so soft that the dominant note was of sibilation (hissing). Her hands, too, were peculiar – long, flexible, white, with a strange movement as of waving gently to and fro.' As if she were about to strike?

Finally, Adam Salton realized that it was his duty to get rid of her, and he destroyed the deep worm-hole with her inside it, using dynamite to blow her into fragments.

'From this the agonized shrieks were rising, growing ever more terrible with each second that passed. Some of these fragments were covered with scaled skin as of a gigantic lizard or serpent. The whole surface of the fragments, once alive, was covered with insects, worms and vermin of all kinds. The sight was horrible enough, but with the awful smell added, was simply unbearable. The worm's hole appeared to breathe forth death in its most repulsive form.'

Married to a mermaid

A jolly Victorian music hall song tells the story of 'a young feller who fell overboard among the sharks and whales' and sinks to the bottom of the ocean, where he meets a mermaid and falls in love with her:

'She raised herself on her beautiful tail,
And gave him her wet white hand,
Saying, "Long have I waited for you, my dear,
You're welcome safe to land.
Go back to your messmates for the last time,
And tell them all from me,
That you're married to a mer-mi-ed
At the bottom of the deep blue sea."'

We think of mermaids as being attractive creatures, but they were also believed to be monsters luring sailors to their deaths, like the Sirens whose songs enticed seafarers to steer their ships on to the rocks. Indeed, the combs with which mermaids are frequently pictured may have been musical instruments like lyres, to bewitch the sailors into coming nearer.

A different interpretation of the mermaid's comb and round-shaped mirror concerns a Greek sailor who was captured but allowed to sing for the last time before he was put to death. His voice was so beautiful that a dolphin swam close to the ship to listen, just as seals are attracted to music today. Seizing his chance, the Greek sailor jumped overboard and rode away on the dolphin's back, looking like a merman as he was seen in silhouette against the silver sea, with his round shield (the mirror) and his forked spear (the comb).

Though this story sounds fantastic, it is not completely fanciful. In the museum of Thasos, one of the northern Greek islands, there is a small, perfect bas-relief (a shallow sculpture against a background) of the goddess Aphrodite riding on the back of a dolphin, the folds of her dress obscuring part of the animal so that she and the dolphin look like one creature with the head of a woman and the tail of a fish. It is known that dolphins have always been friendly towards humans, and if a young girl with long hair was glimpsed on the back of a dolphin they might easily appear to be one creature, especially when seen in silhouette.

The legendary fusion of girl and dolphin was mentioned by Oberon in Shakespeare's *A Mid-Summer Night's Dream*:

'Once I sat upon a promontory
And heard a mermaid on a dolphin's back
Uttering such dulcet and harmonious breath
That the rude sea grew civil at her song
And certain stars shot madly from their spheres
To hear the sea-maid's music.'

In other legends, mermaids are more sinister creatures, and sadder too. They are lost souls who longed to be human beings. The only way they could achieve this was to marry a human, which explains their need to attract sailors towards them.

In Scandinavia, Ireland and Scotland, where the legend is particularly strong, mermaids are often referred to as seal maidens. In one tale, from Scotland, a young man fell in love with a mermaid and married her, careful to conceal her enchanted sealskin when they made their home on land. All went well and they lived together happily for many years bearing several children. One day one of her sons discovered the strange skin and showed it to his mother. She put it on and swam out to sea, leaving her family forever – for once the secret of a mermaid is betrayed, she has to return to the water.

This is a Victorian song sheet cover for 'Married to a Mermaid', originally sung by Arthur Lloyd. The sailor meets a beautiful mermaid at the bottom of the ocean.

MARRIED TO A MERMAID.

SUNG BY

There is another story of a mermaid in the 6th century who was so desperate to become human that she landed on the Holy Island of Iona off the west coast of Scotland to beg a local monk to help her to gain a soul. When he refused she was forced to return to the ocean. The tears she left behind became the small green pebbles still found on the beaches of Iona today where they are known as 'mermaid's tears'.

During his first voyage, Christopher Columbus the discoverer recorded seeing three mermaids leaping high out of the sea off the coast of Guyana, South America; while the English navigator Henry Hudson saw a mermaid in June 1625 while sailing in search of the North-west Passage, Canada.

In spite of their reputation for dragging sailors to a watery grave – 'I'll drown more sailors than a mermaid can!' cries Shakespeare's Richard III – mermaids were so seductive and romantic that sailors fell in love with them regardless of their fate.

Columbus recorded seeing three mermaids leaping out of the sea off the coast of South America.

The mermaid and the fisherman of Zennor

A handsome, dark young fisherman called Mathew Trewhella lived in the seafaring village of Zennor, on the Cornish coast between St Ives and Land's End in Britain. He was known for his splendid voice, which was so powerful when he sang in church on Sunday that it echoed across the water. A mermaid heard it and fell in love with the sound. Swimming towards it, she found a stream which ran from the hill where the church was, and she made her way upstream to listen more closely. As Mathew came out of the church one morning, he spotted her among the ferns and moss. He was so enchanted by her beauty that he swam with her back down the stream to the bottom of the sea where his singing could be heard for several years afterwards by the fishermen above.

On one occasion a fisherman, who had been one of Mathew's friends, dropped his anchor nearby, but the mermaid came to the surface and asked him to leave them alone because Mathew and his new family were living contentedly in a nearby cave.

If you visit the parish church at Zennor today you will find a small carving of a mermaid with glass and comb on one of the oak pews.

The mermaid who took her revenge

The mermaid is such an enchantress that men easily fall for her spells, but underneath she is selfish and torn with jealousy when crossed in love. Another Scottish legend tells of a mermaid who was so infatuated with a young man on the mainland that she gave him a present of gold and silver which she had rescued from a wreck.

The young Scot accepted her presents eagerly, but made the fatal mistake of giving the jewellery to his girlfriend on land.

The carving of a mermaid on the church pew at Zennor in Cornwall.

Instead of keeping away from the mermaid after that, he met her again. She promised to take him to a cave where she had stored all the treasure that had been wrecked over the years in the estuary. Her promise was true, but as he stepped inside, dazzled by a pile of glistening, polished diamonds at the entrance, she slipped a golden chain around him and tied him to a rock. From here he was able to watch the treasure-trove, all the wealth he had ever dreamt of, for the rest of his life, trapped by the mermaid forever.

Postscript If you ever wish to identify a mermaid after she has turned into a human being, look at the hem of her dress – it will always be wet.

It was a strange monster, like a seal with a long tail and ferocious teeth.

The Bunyip

This is a mythical Australian water-serpent.

A group of young Aborigine warriors once set out to look for food. They came to the pools in the mud flat beyond the desert of stones, and uncoiled their fishing lines. Most of them dug up worms for bait, but the chief's son took a piece of raw meat which he had brought for his dinner, and put it on his hook.

The young men didn't catch any fish, and thought they would have to go home empty-handed, when suddenly the chief's son saw his line sink in the water. The others rushed over to help him, and they all pulled hard on the line, landing his catch at last. It was a strange monster, like a seal with a long tail and ferocious teeth. 'It is a Bunyip!' they cried, for their grandparents had warned them of it. 'It is a little Bunyip, the cub of the Great Bunyip! Fling it back quickly!'

But the chief's son would not fling it back. He had promised the maiden he loved that he would bring home food for her family. They couldn't eat the Bunyip, but it would be a plaything for her young brothers and sisters.

Suddenly there was a terrible wailing from behind the pool. Out of her den came the mother Bunyip, rushing towards them, her terrible yellow eyes flashing. The chief's son flung his spear at her, throwing the little Bunyip over his shoulder and running for home with his friends.

They ran and ran, but heard a strange noise behind them. The water from the pool had risen and was flowing towards them! All the plain was covered with water, and it was washing over the trees. The young men quickly ran on up the hill to their village, but the water climbed the hill behind them.

The chief's son let the Bunyip go and caught hold of the girl he loved, for whom he had caught the Bunyip. 'I will save you,' he cried, scrambling up the nearest tree. Suddenly his feet felt cold. He looked down, and they had been turned to webbed feet. He looked at the girl in his arms – she had turned into a black swan. His friends had all become swans too. Suddenly he and the girl were swimming side by side in the water. And that was how black swans came about.

The little Bunyip was carried safely home by the mother Bunyip, and the water returned to its rightful place. Never again has there been so big a flood.

Chapter Five

Hairy Monsters and Hairy Men

Whatever it was it was not a human being, not a bear, not any species of monkey known to exist in Asia.

Eric Shipton

A baby mammoth which weighs 90 kg (200 lb), has recently been discovered in a remote region of Siberia. It has been dead for 40 000 years, entombed in a river-bed and kept in a state of deep-freeze ever since. Because of this, the frozen infant mammoth is still in a remarkable state of preservation – to such an extent that it may still yield living cells.

This has led to the consideration of one of the most extraordinary and monstrous experiments ever to be made: that the nucleus should be taken from the fertilized egg of a living elephant and be injected into the live cell taken from the dead mammoth.

Then, so the scientists claim, a new creature might be created – 'a Lazarus-like revival of an extinct species' – with the possibility that if the experiment succeeds we may see mammoths walking the earth once again. The prospect of 'frozen zoos' in order to preserve our vanishing species is reassuring in one way, but the risks are terrifying, too. Artificial fertilization encourages the survival of the fittest already, but if scientists achieve the miracle of cloning extinct species, who knows what monsters they may produce? The past draws closer.

When the Northern Hemisphere was covered by ice, the warm-blooded mammals which survived the great catastrophe that killed off the dinosaurs had to adapt to the new conditions. They grew hair for protection; they no longer laid their eggs, which needed the sun to hatch them, but formed them as embryos inside the bodies of the mother – as human beings are born today. These hairy creatures, which roamed Asia and North America during the ice-age or Pleistocene epoch, would strike us as highly monstrous today. The *Megatherium*, for example, was a furry giant sloth 5 m (18 ft) tall. However, these mammals were comparatively recent, becoming extinct thousands rather than millions of years ago. They were so recent, in fact, that human beings lived among them. They included mammoths, mastodons, bison, true horses, sabre-toothed cats, giant wolves, camels, pigs – and human beings. Some of these species are still alive today, though in as different forms as we are from our hairy ancestors.

Mammoths (and mastodons) were a type of elephant. The imperial mammoth reached a shoulder height of 4 m (13·5 ft), but the woolly mammoth was 2·7 m (9 ft), resembling an elephant in a fur coat.

There has been some argument recently over the date of their extinction.

People have assumed that the last mammoth died about 12 000 years ago, but recent tracks found in Siberia, measuring 60 cm (2 ft) across and 45 cm (18 in) long, have raised new doubts. At first it seems hard to believe that there are still areas left unexplored where such creatures could hide, until you examine the strange case of the Tunguska fire-ball which crashed into Siberia on the morning of June 30, 1908. The place where it landed, north of Lake Baykal, was so isolated that not a single person was reported killed, though entire forests were flattened. People living 65 km (40 miles) away were knocked unconscious by the impact and trees were reduced to matchsticks. A woman in England wrote to *The Times* asking why the sky had been so bright shortly after midnight that it was possible to read large print indoors: 'At about one-thirty, the room was quite light, as if it had been day. It would be interesting if anyone could explain the cause of so unusual a sight.' Nobody could, at the time.

It was not until 1927 that an expedition was launched to locate the area, headed by a Russian mineralogist who finally reached a peak where he looked down on the destruction: 'From our observation point no sign of forest can be seen for everything has been devastated and burned, and around the edge of this dead area the young 20-year-old forest growth has moved forward furiously, seeking sunshine and life.'

The point is obvious: if the explosion devastated an area up to 30 km (18 miles) from the central point, without killing a single person, and if it took 20 years before an expedition went there to investigate, how can we dismiss stories of living mammoths as preposterous? Most of the mammoths became extinct because they were hunted down by early man, but this can hardly apply to an area where men are seldom seen. Forest covers 7 million sq km (3 million sq miles) of Siberia, so who knows what creatures it contains?

The Yeti – or Abominable Snowman

We should also be prepared to believe in the survival of the hairy men dressed in animal skins who hunted these animals thousands of years ago. Reports of the yeti – or abominable snowmen – have come from regions like Tibet, as remote as Siberia, vouched for by such distinguished men as the Everest explorers, Eric Shipton and Sir Edmund Hillary. (Yeti is the Tibetan word for 'magical creature'.) Rumours of wild, hairy men living in the snowy mountains have persisted for years.

In 1832, the British Resident Officer in Nepal wrote a scientific paper about a shaggy, black-haired creature standing upright, with no tail, which had frightened his native porters. He did not take their frightened description very seriously, dismissing the 'thing' as a stray orang-utan (the large, long-armed ape usually seen in Borneo and Sumatra, whose name is derived from the Malaysian meaning 'man of the woods'). But as the orang-utan is chestnut-brown red, sometimes almost orange, this hardly fits the reference to 'black hair'.

In 1899, Maj L A Waddell, who served with the Indian Army Medical Corps, saw footprints at a height of 5180 m (17 000 ft) north of Sikkim in the Himalayas, though none of the Tibetans he questioned could identify the animal they came across. He concluded that the rumours of 'so-called hairy wild men' were yellow snow bears.

Shipton (standing far left) and Hillary (seated right) with their team of explorers.

In 1921, on the first reconnaissance expedition to Mount Everest, Lieut-Col Howard-Bury saw an upright figure walking quickly over the snow. This was identified by his Sherpa guide as 'the wild man of the snows', but there was no further evidence.

In 1925, a more detailed sighting came from a Fellow of the Royal Geographical Society at 4572 m (15 000 ft) on the Zemu glacier. He saw a creature 182 m (600 ft) away in a valley. It was like a human being, walking upright and stopping occasionally to uproot or pull up some dwarf rhododendron bushes. It showed up dark against the snow and, as far as I could make out, wore no clothes.'

The upright figure was identified by the Sherpa Guide as 'the wild man of the snows'.

We should be prepared to believe in the survival of hairy people dressed in animal skins. This is a scene from the film *Quest of Fire*.

Paul Freeman saw a Bigfoot and its footprints on 10 June, 1982 in Umatilla National Forest, Washington State, USA.

The most convincing report of all came in 1951, from two British mountaineers, Eric Shipton and Michael Ward. They were climbing at 6000 m (20 000 ft) between Tibet and Nepal when they saw giant footprints in the snow, 45 by 33 cm (18 by 13 in), which they measured alongside Ward's ice-axe. Judging by the condition of the snow, the imprints had been made recently with no time for the sun to melt them. This is vitally important, for the smaller prints of an animal such as a goat will widen dramatically in the sun as they melt at the edges, ending up as large tracks.

Later the explorers noticed another set of prints leading towards a glacier and followed them for nearly 1·6 km (1 mile) before the prints disappeared. This time the men had the luck and initiative to record the prints with photographs, which reveal four or five toes, with two inner toes larger than the rest, and a stride of 75 cm (2·5 ft).

Eric Shipton stated his conclusions in the introduction which he wrote to *The Snowman and Company* by Odette Tchernine:

> 'I was inclined to dismiss the creature as fantasy. But the tracks which Michael Ward and I found, in the Menlung Basin after the Everest Reconnaissance Expedition, were so fresh and showed so clearly the outline and contours of the naked feet that I could no longer remain a sceptic. There could be no doubt whatever that a large creature had passed that way a very short time before, and that whatever it was it was not a human being, not a bear, not any species of monkey known to exist in Asia.'

This was written ten years after the sighting, refuting the theories of the Zoological Society in London that the prints were probably those of a langur monkey or red bear.

In 1970, the mountaineer Don Whillans photographed similar footprints at a height of 3600 m (12 000 ft) on the south face of Annapurna, Nepal, and though he was unable to take a photograph, he believed he saw an 'ape-like creature' in the moonlight.

In 1977, two young mountaineers pitched their tent at 5180 m (17 000 ft) in the Himalayas below a sheer glacier. In the middle of the night they were woken up by a terrible din as something or someone crashed into their camp, knocking over their cooking pans, and growling. They were too alarmed to investigate – though they were probably wiser not to do so. The moment it was light, they went outside and found that only one thing was missing: a carton containing 36 bars of chocolate. Either the intruder had a sweet tooth or it was desperately hungry.

Then they spotted the footprints – more than 30 cm (1 ft) across.

Peter Boardman is one of the mountaineers who climbed Everest in 1975, and is an officer of the British Mountaineering Council, so he knew what he was talking about when he reached the conclusion: 'At such a height one cannot believe a darned thing could exist. To say we were apprehensive when we heard the scuffling and banging outside the tent is to put it mildly. When we bedded down for the night we left our food, which was in rucksacks, outside. The box of chocolate bars the creature went for was covered with a plastic bag.'

His companion, Joe Tasker, added: 'Nothing could exist at that height without food in sub-zero temperatures – yet something did.'

Of course the Yeti, or whatever it was, could have said the same about the mountaineers – they existed too, against all the odds, in these impossible conditions.

We give them names, like the Abominable Snowman, but do these creatures really exist? The British medical journal, *The Lancet*, leaves the possibility open: 'Even in the 20th century there are many thinly populated and almost unexplored regions of the world, and in several of these there have arisen rumours of the existence of large animals still awaiting scientific discovery.'

There may have been genuine mistakes, when observers mistook an orang-utan or red bear for something more human.

There may have been deliberate hoaxes, and at least one of the 'scalps' which are supposed to have come from the Yeti has been exposed as a fake made of goat-hair. Apart from financial reward, native guides would try to please visitors by telling them what they wanted to hear, even fabricating evidence.

No photograph has been taken of the Yeti. And if reports of its size are correct, ranging from 1·5 to 4·5 m (5 to 15 ft) high, it would need a lot of food to survive in the freezing cold 6000 m (20 000 ft) above sea level.

One unlikely explanation suggests that the Yeti are not monkeys but monks who withdrew from civilization to the solitude of distant caves. This is the story of a Capt d'Auvergne, the Curator of the Victoria Memorial near Calcutta, who claimed he was rescued by a 2·7-m (9-ft) tall Yeti when he collapsed from snow-blindness in the Himalayas, and was nursed in a cave until he recovered. He believed the creature belonged to an ancient tribe called Aore which had adapted to the mountain conditions over the years.

Indeed, on all the evidence, or the lack of it, the existence of the Yeti is hardly convincing. Yet perhaps it is asking too much to expect specific proof of a creature which would be frightened and skilled at disappearing at the first hint of danger. It would be hard to trace, lurking in the most remote areas left in the world. But if the Yeti does exist, it may not be alone. Its counterparts could be concealed in other regions bypassed by human beings.

Don Whillans believed he saw an 'ape-like creature' in the moonlight.

Big hairy monsters

The Abominable Snowman has a direct parallel in North America where there have been similar reports of wild men. This creature is known to the Indians as *Bigfoot*; and *Sasquatch* in Canada, meaning 'hairy giant'.

For once there is 'evidence', but it is highly dubious. Bigfoot was filmed running through a forest in California. It had an estimated height of 2 m (6·3 ft) and seems to be looking with alarm at the cameraman, which certainly fits with its reputation of being a shy creature who is afraid of people. However, the more you look at the photo, the more you wonder: Bigfoot could easily be a tall man dressed in a gorilla skin, especially the way it is running away. Many experts have denounced the film as a brilliant hoax; others insist that too many people claim to have seen Bigfoot, or footprints at least, to dismiss the idea out of hand.

Is this a genuine picture of Bigfoot, or a brilliant hoax? It was taken by Roger Patterson in 1967, at Bluff Creek, Northern California, USA. (Photo Patterson/Gimlin, © 1968 Dahinden Fortean Picture Library).

The Minnesota Iceman is another big hairy monster, described by the writer Angus Hall as 'famous in his own right as a monster – and, possibly, as the biggest hoax of the century.' The Minnesota Monster was exhibited in 1967 by Frank Hansen who claimed that a 'man left over from the ice age' had been found preserved in ice in the Bering Strait. Charging a modest admission fee, he hawked the carcass of the monster around the carnivals and sideshows of the USA for 18 months. Then a Belgian scientist, Dr Bernard Heuvelmans, came to inspect the body with his colleague, Ivan Sanderson, who lay on top of the glass lid of the refrigerated coffin in order to make detailed drawings. The two experts were suitably impressed, but they noticed something strange – the monster's right eye had been destroyed by a bullet and the back of his skull had been shattered. Even so, they accepted the monster as a species of man, confirming this in a paper written for the Royal Institute of Natural Sciences in Belgium – *Preliminary note on a specimen preserved in ice; an unknown living hominid.*

Hansen claimed to have shot the monster himself while on a hunting trip.

This caused a sensation, encouraging Frank Hansen to exhibit the monster again, though in 1969 it was billed as our 'Neanderthal ancestor – a creature frozen and preserved forever in a coffin of ice'. The billing was not the only thing that was different: the exhibit was plainly a latex model based on the original. Hansen's claims grew wilder with publicity and in 1970 he claimed that he had shot the monster himself when he was on a hunting trip in the north of Minnesota. He said the creature had fallen into the snow which preserved the dead body until he was able to return and take it back to his deep-freeze two months later. Why he exchanged it for the latex model made for him in Hollywood has never been explained, unless the original was starting to decompose.

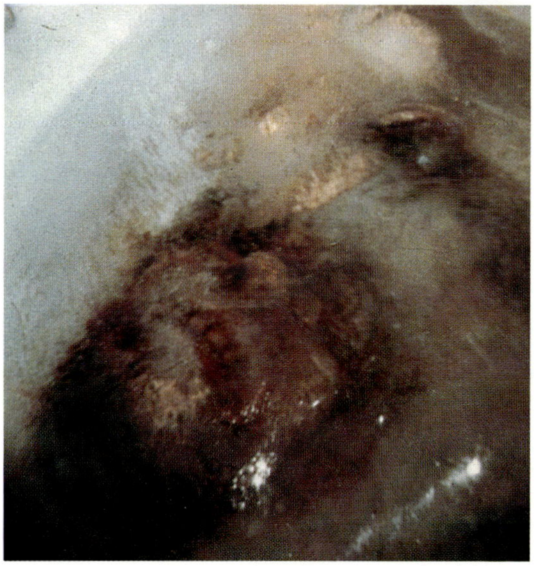

The corpse of the man left over from the ice age which Hansen exhibited.

He saw a 'man-like' creature, walking on its hind legs.

A yell of alarm

Of the thousand case-histories concerning Bigfoot, the earliest remains the most convincing. This was reported in 1851 in a local paper after two hunters in Greene County, Arkansas, saw a creature chasing cattle and described it as 'an animal bearing the unmistakable likeness of humanity'. It was of gigantic stature, the body being covered with hair and the head with long locks that fairly enveloped the neck and shoulders. The 'wild man', after looking at them deliberately for a short time, turned and ran away with great speed, leaping 3·6 to 4·2 m (12 to 14 ft) at a time. His footprints measured 33 cm (13 in).

The newspaper suggested that the beast was a survivor of the local earthquake in 1811, who had reverted to nature and become a wild man of the woods.

Another interesting case was reported by Albert Fletcher in 1917, when he was working at a lumber camp on the Cowlitz River in the state of Washington. He was 17 years old and one evening he was heading for a local dance when he felt that he was being followed. Hiding behind a tree, he saw a large 'man-like' creature, nearly 2·1 m (7 ft) tall, naked though covered with dark hair, and walking on its hind legs. 'Startled, I let out a yell of alarm and the creature instantly turned and ran off into the woods, still on its hind legs.' When the boy told his story, some of the lumberjacks laughed but others said they had seen it too – 'a large ape-like something' resembling a human being.

Romulus and Remus were brought up by wolves.

Wild people in the woods

Stories of wild people who live in the woods and forests date from the time of Nebuchadnezzar, the Babylonian king (605 to 562 BC) who was referred to in the Old Testament Book of Daniel. He was forced to retire into the wilderness during a fit of madness:

> 'He was driven from men, and did eat grass as oxen, and his body was wet with the dew of heaven, till his hairs were grown like eagles' feathers, and his nails like birds' claws.'

This habit of casting mad people adrift to fend on their own continued into the Middle Ages. It was a useful way of getting rid of them, yet gave them a chance as well. Understandably they headed into the heart of the forest where they would be left in peace, and if these wild hairy creatures were spotted by travellers, it is equally understandable that this would lead to stories of wild people, half-animal, half-human.

Nebuchadnezzar, the Babylonian king, was forced to retire into the wilderness during a fit of madness.

It is a story that appeals to the imagination so deeply that it is hard to separate folklore from fact.

Romulus and Remus were the legendary founders of Rome. Mythology claims that they were seized from their mother by a jealous uncle, abandoned, and brought up by wolves.

Rudyard Kipling (1865-1936), an English novelist, told a similar story in *The Jungle Book* (1894). A wood-cutter's child is rescued by a mother wolf who protects the 'man's cub' and persuades the rest of the pack to let him join them. Gradually, Mowgli learns the laws of the jungle, sensitive to 'every rustle in the grass, every breath of the warm night air, every note of the owls above his head . . .' But the young wolves resent his superior intelligence, and at last he is forced to leave them and return to his human family, promising Mother Wolf faithfully that he will come back. 'Come soon,' she tells him, 'little naked son of mine; for listen, child of man, I loved thee more than ever I loved my cubs.'

In real life, Tarzan would have been a hairy monster.

Mowgli is a romantic version of the old tale, and Tarzan, who was brought up by the apes in Africa, is the most glamorous wild man of them all, though in real life he would have been a hairy monster. Is there any truth in the stories of children who have been lost or abandoned and brought up by animals?

The Wolf Boy of Cawnpore

This story has been vouched for by Sir William Christie, who was the City Magistrate of Cawnpore (or Kanpur), India, in the early 1920s when a wolf boy was caught in the jungle ravines near the River Jumna and brought to his court:

> 'He was wild and savage, with spindly legs from the knees downwards, and great long fingernails like claws, and long matted hair. His age was reckoned to be eight to ten. He could not walk, but moved amazingly rapidly on his hands and knees, the latter particularly being hard and gnarled. An orphanage agreed to take the boy, but a large wire cage had to be erected in which to keep him. He would only eat raw meat, which he tore up with his hands and teeth, and of course he could not speak, but only uttered strange and weird noises.'

The boy was transferred to another district in 1924, but Sir William discovered there was another wolf boy in a different orphanage, in his mid or late teens, and went to visit him:

> 'He was in a dormitory with some other boys, but when a stranger like myself entered he scuttled under the nearest bed. But he was already tame by the time I saw him first; the other was still very savage and wild the last time I saw him. Small babies being taken and suckled by wolves was not unknown in northern India at that time, but those were the only two of which I had personal experience.

The remarkable evidence of Sir William Christie should not be doubted, though it might be safer to call them wild boys rather than wolf children, since there is no specific proof that they were suckled by wolves.

These boys would have been able to forage for themselves if they had been abandoned in the jungle. Presenting no threat to the wolves, the packs might even have befriended them so that they learnt the laws of the jungle too and became true children of the wild, tolerated by the rest of the animals if not accepted as one of them.

The Wild Boy of Aveyron

This remarkable story is carefully documented and beyond doubt. The boy had been seen in the woods of southern France and was captured in January 1800, though accounts of his age vary from 12 to 17. Apparently abandoned by his parents, a scar round his throat suggested that they had tried to kill him first, but he found greater kindness with the animals – the wild boar, bears and wolves. A vegetarian, he lived on nuts and roots, was indifferent to the weather and able to move at astonishing speed.

The wild boy of Aveyron found greater kindness when he lived among the animals.

Once he was caught he became an attraction like an animal in a zoo, and was forced into clothes and given food that must have revolted him. Finally he was sent to an institute for the deaf-and-dumb in Paris, where he came to the notice of a brilliant doctor called Jacques Itard. He realized that the wild boy was not the idiot he seemed and became determined to prove this, taking a personal interest in teaching him the rules of civilized society. Gradually the boy learned to stand, mutter sounds, perform a few simple jobs, and this became the subject of a highly successful French film in 1970 called *L'enfant sauvage* (The wild boy), directed by François Truffaut who also played the part of the doctor. The film ended with the doctor's triumphant success, but the truth was more brutal.

Itard stamped out the qualities that the wild boy had gained as an animal, destroying precious gifts of smell, sight and hearing in his determination to make the boy human. When he failed in this attempt, unable to teach the boy human speech, he gave him up after five years and never saw him again. Far from being a benefactor, Dr Itard had been a monster – he had treated the boy callously, leaving him in a halfway state, neither animal nor human, no longer able to return to the privacy of the forest, but unfitted for the public world.

Victor, as the wild boy was called, was looked after by a kindly housekeeper, and it is probable that this simple woman showed him far greater understanding than the brilliant doctor, and gave him love as well. The boy remained an outsider, and he could not be tempted with sweets or alcohol and remained indifferent to fame and power. He had no time for competitive games, either. But when the moon was full, the housekeeper watched him standing for hours looking over the countryside 'in a kind of ecstatic contemplation'. Perhaps he was yearning for his simpler previous life, which may be the reason why stories of wild men appeal to us so strongly, showing an innocence which we have lost. The Wild Boy of Aveyron continued to live with the loving Madame Guérin, who acted as his guardian until he died at the age of 40.

Werewolves

Imagine how easily the rumours would spread if a wild boy reared by wolves grew into a wild man and was seen galloping through the forest with a pack of wolves. People would return with wild stories of a monster or a werewolf. It seems incredible today, but in his *Book of werewolves* (1865), the English clergyman, Sabine Baring Gould, claimed that, 'Half the world believes in or believed in werewolves.'

There seems to be something about the wolf as a symbol of strength which encourages people to believe in werewolves, in spite of the obvious explanations that the rumours really concerned a real wolf, a wild man brought up with the animals, or even one of the unfortunate lunatics who were cast away by society, whose hair grew long and who survived by catching small animals for food.

In France in the 16th and 17th centuries, there was an epidemic of werewolves equal to that of vampirism in Eastern Europe, with 30 000 cases of werewolves listed between 1520 and 1630.

The wish to become a wolf or werewolf is hard to understand. In the past people might have been motivated by reasons of personal revenge, entering into a pact with the devil as witches used to do. Then elaborate rituals would be held at midnight by the light of a full moon, with the would-be-wolf drawing a circle and lighting a fire inside it to heat a cauldron of magic potions and herbs. After smearing his body with animal fat, he would start the incantation, chanting, 'Hail, hail, hail, great wolf spirit, hail! A boon I ask thee, mighty shade. Within this circle I have made, make me a werewolf strong and bold, the terror alike of young and old.' If the mumbo-jumbo was carried out correctly, the candidate was supposed to change into a form 'of a tall, thin monstrosity, half-human and half-animal, grey and nude, with very long legs and arms, and the feet and claws of a wolf.'

The Wild Beast of Exmoor

For centuries there have been legends and rumours of ghostly black dogs which haunt the desolate moors of Devon (see *The Hamlyn Book of Ghosts*, Chapter Two). Other big black dogs have been reported throughout Britain but the West Country is their favourite lurking-ground and it is probable that Conan Doyle based his famous Sherlock Holmes story, *The Hound of the Baskervilles*, on such tales.

There is even a small Devonshire village called Blackdog, with a Black Dog Inn named after a creature which is supposed to have emerged from a tunnel stretching from a medieval mound known as Bury Castle, at the Crossroads to Crediton and Exeter. The famous Black Dog of Torrington was seen on the road to Bideford; while a skeleton hound ran ahead of a phantom coach built from the bones of the four husbands of Lady Howard whose ghost sat inside as it raced along the old road from Tavistock to Okehampton Castle. At Dean Combe in South Devon you can find the Pool of the Black Hound where a weaver was cursed, transformed into a dog and condemned to empty the pool with a leaking walnut shell before he found eternal rest.

Such is the stuff of legends. Suddenly they came alarmingly to life in 1983. It started with rumours of a big cat – 'the British equivalent of the tiger or mountain lion' – reported by the writer and naturalist, Di Francis, who has been pursuing such an animal for years for her book *Cat Country* (1983). In January she found prints of a large animal near the Devon village of Tedburn St Mary which she claimed were made by 'a Dartmoor big cat'.

It is a curious fact that when someone reports seeing a wild 'beast', others suddenly remember they have seen something similar. A woman who works on a farm near Crediton said she had seen such a creature two years earlier: 'like a lioness standing with its paws on the old milk-stand – it had a long tail like an enormous cat.' A farmer, John Anthony, saw a similar beast at midnight: 'Suddenly we shone our torches and there in front of us were two great, glowing eyes. Then the animal turned its head and loped away. We could see that it was a very large, black, cat-like creature.'

Many people thought that the answer was a panther or puma which had escaped from a zoo and returned to the wild. Investigating one of the pawprints on Dartmoor, the journalist Douglas Orgill was reminded of some he had seen four years earlier in Nepal – of a tigress.

Then, at the start of the lambing season, there were new reports from Exmoor and this time there was the irrefutable evidence of slaughtered lambs, nearly eighty in a few weeks, their bodies ripped from the throat to the hindquarters. 'The beast kills and eats a lamb like no dog or fox ever did,' said a local farmer, Denys Smaldon. 'It pulls the wool away and attacks the shoulder and rump. This thing eats the wool as well and leaves the bone structure of the neck, like you would leave a fishbone in a restaurant.'

By now it was known as 'The Beast of Exmoor'. A Sunday paper drew an Identi-Cat, and 12 Royal Marine Commandos who were super-snipers were sent into the area around South Molton with night-vision equipment to try to shoot the beast.

There was growing alarm as one farmer lost £2000 after 40 of his ewes were killed; and three valuable sheep dogs were shot by mistake.

At the end of May, Mrs Doreen Lock saw the beast in daylight as she drove from the Black Cock Inn to the Exmoor village of Molland: 'I saw something in the road – it was large, dark and had pricked ears. Then it disappeared into the wood.' She had seen nothing like it before. The undergrowth near Drewstone Farm where she saw the beast was growing dense. It seemed likely that the animal would escape for another year at least.

What is it? Most people favour a large, wild dog, but Di Francis says the lambs have been scalped 'and a dog chews bones, but these are not touched.' Could it be a puma or panther? This seems a likely explanation until one remembers the Surrey puma which was reported hundreds of times in the 1960s but always escaped capture. A natural wild cat? The scientists remain doubtful, claiming that such an animal would have been caught by now. Is it just conceivable that the black dogs and the Wild Beast of Exmoor are phantoms – memories of the past? The carcasses of eighty lambs prove otherwise. The mystery continues.

The wild beast of Exmoor is probably an escaped panther or a puma.

'This nameless and horrible monster'

The journalist Ed Malone went on the expedition led by Professor Challenger, the famous zoologist, to South America in his search of the 'lost world' which had been bypassed by time. After sighting such apparently extinct species as the *Pterodactyl*, Malone climbed to the top of a tree in order to spy out the land, and found himself staring into a face that was 'far more human than any monkey's that I have ever seen.' That night, Malone strayed from the camp in spite of the danger that this apparent ape-man – 'this nameless and horrible monster' – might spring out from the shadows and attack him. Malone realized he was lost when he saw the reflections of lights on the lake which he had named Gladys Lake, after his girlfriend back in London. To begin with, he was puzzled by the lights which resembled port-holes in a gigantic liner, until he realized they were fires in caves along the shore – and must have been lit by people. 'There were human beings, then, upon the plateau. How gloriously my expedition was justified! Here was news indeed for us to bear back to London.'

Gulliver was cast ashore and discovered by the tiny people of Lilliput.

Lord Roxton could be describing the Bigfoot . . . but of course this is pure fiction, a continuation of Conan Doyle's imaginary exploration of *The Lost World.* Also, Doyle's combination of primitive man alongside prehistoric animals like *Pterodactyls*, is an impossibility, for human beings did not live until a much later date, unless the experts are mistaken. Doyle's ape-man, however, half-animal and half-human, is a favourite theme of storytellers. One of the greatest was Jonathan Swift, who described equally revolting creatures in *Gulliver's Travels* (1726).

Swift was a brilliant satirist who recognized the ironies of life and mocked the hypocrisies of the early 18th century. To begin with, it was Gulliver who was the monster after he was cast ashore and discovered by the tiny people of Lilliput who were no more than 15 cms (6 ins) tall, compared to his height which was truly monstrous by their standards. 'It's a monster – a giant!' they screamed, when they set eyes on him, and they referred to him as a monster throughout.

In fact there were two tribes which lived at opposite ends of the plateau in a constant state of war: the 'nameless and horrible monster' – the ape-men; and the more human form of primitive man. Ed Malone hurried back to the camp to alert the others, but was told by Lord John Roxton, a famous Amazonian explorer who had joined the expedition, that they had been captured by the ape-men though he managed to escape. He told Malone what had happened:

> 'I shot one of them through the belly, but before we knew where we were they had us spread-eagled on our backs. I call them apes, but they carried sticks and stones in their hands and jabbered talk to each other, and ended up by tyin' our hands with creepers, so they are ahead of any beast I have seen in my wanderin's. Ape-men – that's what they are – missin' links, and I wish they'd stayed missin'. They carried off their wounded comrade – he was bleedin' like a pig – and then they sat around us, and if I ever saw frozen murder it was in their faces. They were big fellows, as big as a man and a deal stronger. Curious glassy grey eyes they have, under red tufts, and they just sat and gloated and gloated.'

This artist's impression of Gulliver appeared in an early 18th-century edition of *Gulliver's Travels.*

The monstrous Yahoos

On a subsequent voyage to the country of the Houyhnhnms, Gulliver was threatened by his mutinous crew who rowed him ashore and dumped him on a coral strand – as a sailor, Gulliver seems to have been particularly unlucky. With no idea where he was, Gulliver set off in the hope of finding out, and spotted some animals sitting in a tree. These were the monstrous Yahoos:

> 'Their heads and breasts were covered with a thick hair, some frizzled and others lank; they had beards like goats, and a long ridge of hair down their backs, and the fore parts of their legs and feet; but the rest of their bodies were bare, so that I might see their skins which were of a buff colour. They had no tails, nor any hair at all on their buttocks . . . Upon the whole, I never beheld in all my travels so disagreeable an animal, or one against which I naturally conceived so strong an apathy.'

The monstrous Yahoos: 'I never beheld in all my travels so disagreeable an animal.'

He followed a track in the hope of finding some natives, when he came face to face with one of these creatures:

> 'The ugly monster, when he saw me, distorted several ways every feature of his visage, and stared, as at an object he had never seen before; then, approaching nearer, lifted up his forepaw, whether out of curiosity or mischief, I could not tell: but I drew my hanger, and gave him a good blow with the flat side of it; for I durst not strike him with the edge, fearing that the inhabitants might be provoked against me, if they should come to know, that I had killed or maimed any of their cattle. When the beast felt the smart, he drew back, and roared so loud, that a herd, of at least forty, came flocking about me from the next field, howling and making odious faces.'

Gulliver ran to a tree for protection, but several of the appalling Yahoos climbed up the branches and used him, underneath, as an outside lavatory! 'I escaped pretty well,' Gulliver recounted, 'by sticking close to the stem of the tree, but was almost stifled with the filth; which fell about me on every side.'

Gulliver was rescued by a horse, which puzzled him at first because it seemed an exceptionally intelligent animal, until he realized that horses were the rulers of this land. For a moment he wondered if they were really magicians who had transformed themselves into equine form, scarcely able to believe in the superiority of animals, but soon he threw himself on their mercy: 'I am a poor distressed Englishman, driven by his misfortunes upon your coast,' and he listened closely as they talked among themselves, making out the word 'Yahoo' which was repeated several times. Gradually he understood that the horses were the Houyhnhnms and the revolting creatures were the Yahoos – and then, to his absolute horror, that they considered *him* a Yahoo too!

The noble, courageous Gulliver – a Yahoo. The idea was unthinkable, but as if to prove it the horses took him to a courtyard where they compared him to one of these 'detestable creatures', and the resemblance is confirmed in spite of Gulliver's clothes. Gulliver took a closer look:

> 'My horror and astonishment are not to be described, when I observed, in this abominable animal, a perfect human figure; the face of it, indeed, was flat and broad, the nose depressed, the lips large, and the mouth wide; but these differences are common to all savage nations . . .'

With sly mockery of European society, Swift made Gulliver feel the same revulsion that a Duchess might have felt on being confronted with a number of the so-called 'lower classes'. Because he was intelligent and learned their language, the Houyhnhnms took a liking to Gulliver and gave him preferential treatment, though they continued to treat him much like the Yahoo for which he felt such contempt. Indeed, their kindness made Gulliver feel mortified as he remembered how horses were treated in England as beasts of burden to be ridden and whipped. In fact the more he told them about his own country, the more he shocked them with his accounts of war, greed and stupidity which were so alien to their own gentler nature. By comparison, the human-like Yahoos were wholly dreadful, hating one another and seizing everything for themselves without a thought of sharing it. The Yahoos fought for shining stones, which they collected as jewels, and for roots which they sucked with delight for this 'produced the same effect that wine hath upon us.'

Swift was making it plain that the Yahoos were just like ourselves, and that compared to the innocence displayed by animals, mankind is monstrous.

Gulliver threw himself on the mercy of the horses.

Postscript Recently there has been an astonishing resurgence of interest in both the Loch Ness Monster and the Yeti, as if we are nearing the end of the trail.

A new claim suggests that a race of hairy humans, rather than animals, are still breeding in remote parts of Asia today. These are not ordinary human beings but a throwback to the original, hairy cavemen known as *Neanderthals* who may not have become extinct 35 000 years ago when our ancestors invaded their hunting territories, as people have assumed.

The name *Neanderthal* comes from the skeleton found in a cave in the Neander valley near Dusseldorf in Germany in 1866, our closest link with the past. Neanderthals failed to develop and supposedly died out while human beings flourished.

Consequently, the claim that they still exist is sensational. It is made by Dr Myra Shackley, a lecturer in archaeology at Leicester University, who says creatures with protruding brows only able to communicate with whistling sounds, have been seen in southern China. This echoes the description of a creature found by the Russian explorer V A Khaklov at the start of this century: 'They are of medium height, with hair all over their bodies. They have no forehead but prominent brow-ridges and heavy lower jaw and no chin; with long arms and short legs. The feet are broad, with the big toe shorter than the others, but massive and projecting inwards, with the other toe fanned out.' It is tempting to assume this must have been an ape.

There was an unfortunate incident around 1925 when a Russian general was chasing bandits through the Pamir Mountains and one of his soldiers shot a wild creature when it emerged from a cave. The accompanying doctor examined the creature and at first glance he thought it *was* an ape, heavily covered in hair. But he knew that there were no apes in that district and decided it was definitely human – 'The teeth were large and even and shaped exactly like human teeth.' He identified the body as male, elderly, and 1·6 to 1·7 m (5·5 ft) tall. 'The creature had a very powerful chest and well developed muscles. *We didn't find any important anatomical differences between it and man.*' It was bad enough that armed men killed it in the first place, but then they foolishly buried the body under a tomb of stones which has never been rediscovered.

However, there have been several sightings of *almas* (the Mongolian word for wild-men) since then. Tribesmen of the Kirghiz district were used to seeing these harmless creatures

who lived in caves and survived on berries and small animals. In 1963, a doctor saw an entire family of *almas* in the Altai mountains, and in 1974 a shepherd met a group of them in the mountains of south-west Mongolia: 'half-men and half-beasts with reddish-black hair . . . The size of a medium height man, the *almas* walks with his knees bent, stoops and is pigeon-toed. He has broad shoulders and long arms; his big toe sticks out. *Almas* are easily frightened and suspicious, though not aggressive, and lead a nocturnal life. No one has ever heard them speak. They are usually to be seen at dawn and at dusk and are believed to live on roots, leaves, grass and other vegetation. They prefer to stay in places far away from man, in mountains, for instance.'

You can make your own choice. Weighing the evidence, it is impossible to say with any certainty that a form of primitive man inhabits these remote regions in Asia. But enough people have seen such a creature to suggest that *something* unfamiliar exists out there.

Perhaps it would spoil the guessing-game if any explorer found out what *it* is.

'Presently came other glimpses of lurking semi-human shapes and grey forms that ran in the twilight.'

(*The Grisly Folk*, H G Wells)

Dr Myra Shackley claims that Neanderthal cave people may not have become extinct after all.

Chapter Six

People on Show

We hold that any being with a soul should be respected.

Theophile Gautier

Giants

Through a quirk of fate, it often happens that ordinary people are trapped inside extra-ordinary bodies. Obvious examples are those who are born too tall or too small – giants and midgets. They are facts of life and are not to be condemned for their unusual size, but giants are also a part of mythology.

In Norse mythology, the gigantic Ymir was the first man on earth and created the human race. The Indians of north-west America believed in stories of primeval giants who were cannibals; while in Greek mythology there are titans and gigantes.

In British mythology there are the little people – pixies, elves and fairies; and at the other end of the scale there is the legend that the island was inhabited by 5 m (18 ft) giants until they were defeated by the Trojan Brutus. He conquered Britain and seized the last surviving giants, Gog and Magog, bringing them to London to serve humiliatingly as porters at the gates of the Guildhall.

Myths concerning these two giants were widespread: the hills behind Cambridge are known as the Gogmagog Hills and include a Celtic fort which is associated with a legend of an early giant.

Because he symbolized great strength, the downfall of a giant has become a popular theme in folklore and pantomimes, such as *Jack the giant-killer* or *Jack and the beanstalk*. These, and the biblical tale of David and Goliath, may have been based on fact, even though the champion of the Philistines was alleged to be 'six cubits and a span' which is almost 3 m (10 ft) tall. Such unnatural height would have weakened

Goliath, quite apart from his heavy armour of chain-mail which weighed 94 kg (208 lb), so a boy could have accepted his challenge to the Israelites, toppling the cumbersome giant with a stone from his sling.

Other legends are more fantastic, like the creation of the Wrekin hill in Shropshire.

The giant who lost his way

A Welsh giant had such a grievance against the mayor of Shrewsbury that he decided to take his revenge. He planned to dam the River Severn in order to flood the city and drown the people. He headed towards the Severn with a vast shovel of earth, but he lost his way. He met a cobbler who was returning from Shrewsbury with a bag full of old shoes which he had collected for mending. The giant called down to him, asking how far it was to Shrewsbury.

He met a cobbler who was returning from Shrewsbury with a bag full of old shoes.

Quickly realizing the danger the city was in, with the possible loss of his customers, the cobbler assured the giant that he would not arrive there that day, or even the next. The giant looked so surprised that the cobbler opened his bag in proof: 'Look! I've come from Shrewsbury myself and worn out all these shoes on the way.'

The giant, who was stupid by comparison, scratched his head with bewilderment and then lost heart, throwing his shovelful of earth on the ground beside him – and creating the Wrekin.

Other landmarks bearing such names as the Giant's Leap, or the Giant's Causeway in County Antrim in Northern Ireland, are further tributes to the strength of giants who made islands by hurling rocks into the sea, or valleys by lying down to rest. And though the size and strength of the giants must have grown larger each time these stories were told, there is good reason to believe that tribes of tall men did exist. On Lundy Island in the Bristol Channel, west of Ilfracombe, a grave was unearthed containing the skeletons of men at least 2·4 m (8 ft) tall, covered with limpet shells; while the Masai people in Kenya today are exceptionally handsome and of unusual height.

A few giants held positions of power, like the Roman Emperor Maximinius who was 2·4 m (8 ft) tall; and some were perfectly formed, like a man called Hales who was 1·9 m ($6\frac{1}{2}$ ft) and married a woman not much shorter than himself. They had four sons and five daughters, all over 1·8 m (6 ft), and one of the sons, Robert Hales, became known as 'The Norfolk giant'. He was 2·3 m ($7\frac{1}{2}$ ft) tall, and was presented to Queen Victoria in 1851. He worked as the landlord of a public house in Drury Lane and led a reasonably normal life.

Other giants were less fortunate and suffered the humiliation of being forced into circus acts. There is something demeaning about a large man appearing with a 'mermaid' or Siamese twins as the showman Barnum made them do, and some were understandably sensitive. A gentle giant called Patrick Cotter, billed as 'The celebrated Irish giant, indisputably the tallest man ever shown', was terrified that his body would be dug up after his death. Dying in Bristol, he was buried 3·6 m (12 ft) into the rock and his coffin was enclosed by iron bars. His fear was justified, for the body of another giant was vandalized and his skeleton sold to an anatomist for eight hundred pounds, ending up as an exhibit in the Royal College of Surgeons of England, where it still is.

The midget who jumped from a pie

The English aristocracy was equally obsessed with small people. A midget called Jeffrey Hudson, who was 45 cm (18 in) high, was presented to the Duke of Buckingham when he was nine years old by his father, a local butcher, and even jumped out of a pie when Charles I and Queen Henrietta were entertained to dinner.

He became so celebrated that he joined the queen's court as a favourite. He was sent to France in 1630 but was seized by pirates and only released after the payment of a ransom. Hudson was braver than you would expect from his size, fighting with the army and protecting the queen when she fled to Paris. He challenged an Englishman who made a joke about his tiny appearance. To add to this insult, the man arrived for the duel with a water-pistol, which prompted Hudson to call for real pistols and shoot him dead. Forced to escape from Paris, Hudson was captured by Turkish pirates but finally reached England again, where he was foolish enough to be involved in a plot against the king. He was caught and sentenced to prison, but all was forgiven before his death in 1682. He received a royal pardon and a generous gift of money from Charles II.

Even the most misshapen dwarfs were given their opportunities, such as Mathew Buckinger who was 73 cm ($2\frac{1}{2}$ ft) tall with no legs or arms and flipper-like growths on his shoulders instead of hands. In spite of this disability, he became extraordinarily skilled at drawing, and examples of his work are preserved in the British Museum, London. He married four times and had eleven normal children.

In the 18th century, the British preoccupation with dwarfs was described as 'reaching the proportions of a disease'. But at least their aristocratic patronage spared dwarfs and midgets the humiliation of the fairgrounds, where less fortunate people were cruelly paraded as freaks.

The shows at Bartholomew Fair

The most famous fair was Bartholomew's Fair at Smithfield, later London's meat market. Writing to his son in 1685, a man complained about the monsters he saw there: 'Others born in any monstrous shape, or having children as such, here celebrate their misery, and, by getting of money, forget how odious they are made.'

Attractions included an Indian dwarf, 76 cm ($2\frac{1}{2}$ ft) high, known as 'The little old woman of Baghdad'; and 'A wonder of nature', the 15-year-old Cheshire girl who was only 45 cm (18 ins) high – 'She never had a perfect bone in any part of her, only the head, yet she hath all her senses and discourses, reads very well, sings and whistles, and all very pleasant to hear.' These were exhibited in 1825.

Competitions were held for the tiniest human alive, and when Charles Dickens visited Greenwich Fair in 1835 he referred to the dwarfs as 'objects of great curiosity'. Though he mentioned a living skeleton, a wild Indian, a beautiful young lady with white hair and pink eyes (obviously an albino), and a celebrated pig-faced woman, it was the dwarf who caught the writer's attention: 'The best thing about a dwarf is, that he has always a little box, about two feet six inches high'. This was painted outside like an ordinary house, supposedly containing six rooms which the dwarf lived in. Once he was squeezed inside, he fired a pistol from 'the first floor window', and the crowds really believed that this was his home.

Always a compassionate observer, Dickens sympathized with the 'unfortunate little object' shut up in his box, and remarked that it was not surprising that the dwarf was 'always particularly drunk'.

The most popular midget in history

In the last century, when people were more gullible, the greatest showman of them all was Phineas T Barnum, who gloated as he raked in the coins: 'There's a sucker born every minute!' Fake monsters were big business at shows and fairs. Mermaids were especially popular, and Barnum attracted his customers with paintings of beautiful creatures displayed on the tent outside. When they ventured inside they must have been disappointed even if they failed to realize they were the victims of a hoax, for instead of finding mermaids swimming about in a tank they were met by a hideous, decaying corpse made from the top half of a dead monkey joined to the tail of a fish.

Barnum discovered a boy called Charles Stratton in Bridgeport, Connecticut in 1832. The moment he set eyes on the boy, who was 63 cm (2 ft) high, Barnum sensed that a foreign background would make him more mysterious and launched him in New York as General Tom Thumb, visiting from England. The name was a stroke of genius and assured their success. In due course, Tom Thumb did go to England where they hoped he would be received by Queen Victoria, but the court was officially in mourning for Prince Albert's father. When he was told Barnum quickly spread the rumour that he was leaving England to present the general to Louis Philippe, King of France, which is why Queen Victoria, who wanted to see him first, broke with tradition.

This poster of Phineas T Barnum appeared in the American magazine *Vanity Fair*.

By this time, Tom Thumb was a remarkable entertainer. He danced a nautical hornpipe before the queen, imitated Greek statues, and gave an impersonation of Napoleon which 'elicited great mirth' among the British, who had defeated Napoleon and his armies. When he was presented to the Duke of Wellington, the hero of the Battle of Waterloo asked what Tom Thumb was thinking of when he posed as his enemy Napoleon, and received the prompt reply, 'I was wondering why I lost the battle.'

Queen Victoria was delighted and gave Tom Thumb a present of jewels and money, but her royal approval was even more valuable in terms of publicity. Londoners flocked to see Tom Thumb in the Egyptian Hall in such thousands that a rival exhibitor, showing his paintings in another room which no one went to, shot his brains out after leaving this entry in his diary: 'They rush by thousands to see Tom Thumb. They push, they fight, they scream, they faint, they cry "help!" and "murder!" They see my posters but do not read them . . . It is insanity.'

Exploiting the royal patronage, Barnum paid the queen's carriage-maker to build a miniature chariot for Tom. This was lined with yellow silk inside, with the general's coat of arms, which Barnum designed himself on the outside – Liberty and Britannia, supported by an eagle and a lion.

Charles Stratton was notorious as he and Barnum made their triumphal tour across Europe, but the French novelist Theophile Gautier described the general as 'a little monster'. Criticizing the adoration he was receiving in France, Gautier protested: 'These medical curiosities should be confined to medical amphitheatres and the apothecary's jar. We

Tom Thumb married Lavinia Warren, another dwarf, in 1863 in New York. The wedding was a national event, and another dwarf, Cmdr Nutt, was best man.

hold that any being with a soul should be respected. Nature occasionally makes a mistake, why cause it to blush for its errors and miscarriages?'

Stratton managed to have a private life as well, though even this was all too public. His marriage to another midget, Lavinia Warren, in 1863, was turned into a national event. Barnum gained maximum publicity from the rivalry between Tom Thumb and Cmdr Nutt, a younger, more handsome midget, with whom Lavinia had been touring. But Tom Thumb's fame won the day, Lavinia married him and Nutt agreed to be their best man. The ceremony at New York's Grace Church was attended by celebrities inside and hysterical crowds without, and filled the front pages of the newspapers instead of the latest news of the Civil War. Two nights later, Gen and Mrs Thumb were presented to President Lincoln at the White House, then the couple sailed again for Europe where they were welcomed by Queen Victoria.

There is little doubt that Barnum exploited Tom Thumb shamefully, but exploitation was his business. He made Tom a fortune and the midget remained loyal to him, helping out with a farewell tour which recouped Barnum's money after he had suffered a financial setback.

Tom Thumb was rich when he died in 1883, but his investments fell afterwards and his widow was forced to go back on tour. She ended up on Coney Island, New York, in a seedy side-show as 'a freak among freaks', a pitiful end after her triumphs with Tom Thumb.

At least Lavinia Thumb had enjoyed a happy marriage, but love affairs between a midget and someone of normal size were seldom successful, with more than the usual share of problems.

Romances which could not last

In 1929 a young man fell in love with one of the most exquisite midgets of the century, a Miss Lili Dantini, a Hungarian singer aged 28 who was under 1·2 m (4 ft) tall. She was cautious at first, but when she was convinced that his love was genuine she agreed to marry him in three months' time. By now she was in love too, but the interval gave her time to think of their future together, and she wrote him this poignant letter when she was on tour: 'You must have known that it could not last. You love me now, but you would soon grow ashamed of having a freak for your wife, and you would loathe me. It is best that we forget our marriage plans – some day you will thank me. Lili.' She possessed the wisdom of foresight, and considerable courage too.

The birthday of the infanta

It was the Infanta of Spain's 12th birthday and a dwarf was brought to the Spanish court for her party. He had been seen running wild in the woods by hunters two days earlier, and his father, a poor charcoal burner, was glad to be rid of his useless, ugly child. But 'even for the Spanish court, always noted for its cultivated passion for the horrible, so fantastic a little monster had never been seen.'

At least the 'little monster' was a constant source of amusement:

'Perhaps the most amusing thing about him was his complete unconsciousness of his own grotesque appearance. Indeed he seemed quite happy and full of the highest spirits. When the children laughed, he laughed as freely and as joyously as any of them, and at the end of each dance he made them each the funniest of bows, smiling and nodding at them just as if he was really one of themselves, and not a little misshapen thing that nature, in some humorous mood, had fashioned for others to mock him. As for the infanta, she absolutely fascinated him.'

'Why had they not left him in the forest, where there was no mirror to tell him how ugly he was?'

Later, the happy dwarf made a terrible mistake when he went into a strange room and saw something moving. For a moment he thought it must be the infanta, then the figure moved again and he was appalled:

> 'It was a monster, the most grotesque monster he had ever beheld. Not properly shaped as all other people were, but hunchbacked and crooked limbed, with a huge lolling head and mane of black hair. He laughed, and it laughed with him, and held its hands to its sides, just as he was doing. He made a mocking bow, and it returned him a low reverence.
>
> 'When the truth dawned on him, he gave a wild cry of despair, and fell sobbing to the ground.'

The monster was himself, seen in a mirror for the first time.

> 'So it was he who was misshapen and hunchbacked, foul to look at and grotesque. He himself was the monster, and it was at him that all the children had been laughing, and the little princess who he had thought loved him – she too, had been merely mocking at his ugliness, and making merry over his twisted limbs. Why had they not left him in the forest, where there was no mirror to tell him how loathsome he was?'

The infanta entered the room with her courtiers, who burst into laughter when they saw the dwarf in despair beating the ground with his fists.

> 'His dancing was funny,' she said, 'but his acting is funnier still.'

But the little dwarf never looked up – he suddenly gave a curious gasp and lay quite still. The chamberlain knelt beside him and told the impatient infanta that her dwarf would never dance again, 'because his heart was broken.'

> 'And the infanta frowned, and her dainty rose-leaf lips curled in pretty disdain. "For the future let those who come to play with me have no hearts," she cried, and she ran out into the garden.'

(*The Birthday of the Infanta*, Oscar Wilde, 1888)

Chapter Seven

Gentle Gorillas

Should the whole human species vanish from the earth tomorrow, there would not be a plant, bird, insect or animal that would not breathe a sigh of relief.

Sir Laurens van der Post

Human beings are the greatest monsters of them all, arrogantly assuming that animals were put on earth for people to kill.

At least there was some justification when human beings killed for food or skins to wear, but lions and tigers, wolves and gorillas were shot purely out of fear – or, even worse, for the fun of it. And this still happens.

New evidence proves that in many ways animals are superior to people in their behaviour; the wolf, for example, mates for life and rears the cubs of any other she-wolf which has been killed. The wolf never attacks human beings unless provoked, while people often kill people with no provocation.

As for the gorilla, few creatures have been so maligned.

Early explorers who glimpsed gorillas in the dense jungles of West Africa can be forgiven for describing them as monsters – they knew no better, never having seen a gorilla before. This was the first impression of Negley Farson (the author's father), who described gorillas in *Behind God's Back* (1940) when he went on a gorilla hunt 2438 m (8000 ft) high in the rain forests of the Congo:

> 'We came upon them among the lobelias. For what reason they had remained, or remained silent, I'll never know. But the moment we reached the rim of that open knoll they began to beat their chests. It's a horrible sound, meant to strike terror into everything in the forest, and it certainly worked with me. That terrible shrill hammering – they don't yell; they just beat the caverns of their chests with their mouths open – hit me like a kick in the stomach.

The natives all leaned back on their right legs, with spears held back, ready to throw them. Then ran. Then I realized they never had any intention of *facing* the animal; it was just, as a last resort, to hurl these things at them – and fly. The bushes within 15 ft (4 m) of us were being whipped about. The gorillas were right *there!* right in front of our eyes! and still we could not see them. Then a bush immediately before me whipped down, and I saw a face staring at me, above a huge, humped shoulder. I set my feet – and the bush whipped back again.

'I could say now that, yes, I have seen a gorilla, I have faced him within 15 ft (4 m) but if I had to draw the picture of a gorilla from what I saw of one – well, it would be as much like a sea-serpent as anything else. Except – for a second it swung its arms! And now I *know* why those pre-Elizabethan explorers brought back tales of serpents with beards, and "King Kong" monsters, and were not able to agree, even on the things they had seen in company. For, having no previous knowledge of, say, anything larger than a monkey – and *then* running on to a gorilla – why, he might have been 20 ft (6 m) high! The sight of him was worse than his shrieks!'

'The gorillas were right there in front of our eyes.'

Negley Farson, the author's father, on safari.

Negley Farson ventured into the jungle to see the gorillas rather than shoot them, and he was a compassionate observer, but the gorillas still looked monstrous to him. He did not realize that they are among the gentlest creatures alive.

Today we are less naive, thanks to television which has broadened our outlook on animals and nature with such series as *Survival* and *The World About Us*.

Who can forget the sight of David Attenborough lying in the middle of a cluster of gorillas when he was filmed for *Life on Earth*, proving once and for all what trusting creatures they are.

Attenborough has described how similar gorillas are to ourselves (*Life on Earth*, 1979): 'Their sight and sense of hearing and smell are closely similar to our own, so that they perceive the world in very much the same way as we do.'

Living in family groups of a dozen or so, gorillas reach the same age as ourselves, when we allow them to. Far from killing for meat,

David Attenborough, filmed during *Life on Earth* (BBC Copyright photograph).

Gorillas, perhaps the closest relatives of human beings, are often killed by poachers.

they are vegetarians, but as the adult males weigh up to 270 kg (600 lb) they seldom climb because the trees are unable to support them. They exist on vegetation within their massive grasp, such as nettles and giant celery, making their beds on the flattened ground afterwards.

The fearsome appearance of the gigantic silver-backed gorilla who leads the pack is deceptive, just as the chest-beating is a warning signal. Otherwise, as Attenborough relates from his first-hand experience: 'They sit quietly grazing, ripping huge handfuls of stems from the ground with slow, irresistible sweeps of their immense hands, lolling among the dense nettles and celery, sometimes grooming one another. Occasionally they exchange quiet grunts or gurgles and if an individual wanders away from the main group it makes a little belching sound every now and then so that the rest know where it is.'

The young gorillas play and wrestle like children, sometimes 'aping' their parents as they rise on their hind legs and beat their chests. David Attenborough was careful to treat them all with courtesy:

> 'A stare is rude, or, put in a less anthropocentric (human) way, threatening – a challenge that invites reprisal. Keeping the head low and the eyes down is a way of expressing submission and friendliness.'

No wonder gorillas have been called the closest relative of human beings. Yet people kill them. Twenty years ago 450 mountain gorillas were left in the wild, but now they are the rarest of the great apes and the figure is estimated at 350 or even less. This is a critical number for their chances of survival. The majority live in a small area of dense forest which lies on the borders of three Central African states: Rwanda, Zaire and Uganda. The danger is that because the gorillas lead a lazy, contented life, harming no one, they are easy victims for poachers, and as the females only give birth after eight years and then have one baby gorilla every four years, any decline in their numbers is serious.

But there is good news too. The Mountain Gorilla Project launched by the Fauna and Flora Preservation Society, which has the support of David Attenborough and the Queen of England, also has the encouragement of the Rwanda Government and this will be crucial to the future survival of the last remaining gorillas. Rwanda is a small country with the densest population in Africa, but there are two national parks which are a valuable tourist attraction and the Park of the Volcanoes, where the gorillas live, is little use for anything else, such as cultivation.

Unless preventive action is taken, gorillas may soon become extinct.

The Gorillas Project is in action already. Believing that the future for the gorilla lies with the present generation of schoolchildren, funds are being raised for a mobile audio-visual unit to be used in schools throughout Rwanda, explaining why the survival of the gorilla is so important. In 1981, the Rwanda government made the export of mountain gorillas illegal and as a result of this new concern the number of young gorillas is beginning to rise.

Even so, the 1980s will probably decide their fate. It is an appalling thought that unless such wildlife organizations as the Gorilla Project succeed, these magnificent 'monsters' may become as dead as the dodo, something to remember from picture books. Should you wish to become involved yourself, the address is: The Gorilla Project – Fauna and Flora Preservation Society, c/o Zoological Society of London, Regent's Park, London NW1 4RY, Great Britain.

Meanwhile, conservationists like Gerald Durrell in Guernsey, and John Aspinall, with his private zoo in Britain, are breeding gorillas in captivity in order to return them to the wild – 'If there is a wild left for them to return to,' adds Durrell, 'which seems unlikely.'

Aspinall, who describes himself as 'an honorary gorilla' when he enters their cage to play, believes, 'It is the dream of every responsible zoo director to repatriate gorillas to their own land.' He is shocked by the indifference of people who say 'So what?' when they are told that the mountain gorilla might soon be extinct: 'What can you do with such apathy?'

The price of a gorilla's hand

Reserves have been set up in Africa where tourists, limited to six at a time, can watch the wild gorillas for a moderate fee. Ironically, such good intentions can have the reverse effect, for just as tourists kill the place they love, so the conservationists have alerted the poachers to the value of gorilla heads and hands as tourist trophies.

In 1978 there was an international outcry when Digit, a lovable 127-kg (280-lb) gorilla was beheaded by a poacher who sold a hand to be used as an ashtray to a trader for 20 dollars. '20 dollars!' exclaimed the American zoologist Dian Fossey, 'for a life beyond value. It is an irreconcilable thought.'

In December 1981 at Rwanda, Central Africa, two rare mountain gorillas were shot and their baby kidnapped. These were part of the same innocent family which sprawled with David Attenborough, lazily and happily in the jungle, watched by millions of television viewers. Scientific observers were anxious when they disappeared from Mount Karisimbi in the National Park of the Volcanoes, and their fears were realized when a dealer was arrested a few days later in the town of Ruhengeri when he tried to sell one of the gorilla's heads to a tourist. Who was the monster here?

The only enemies of such animals are human beings: we shoot them for trophies, skin them, and tear down their forests leaving the survivors less space to live in. Even zoos, apart from the cruelty of cramped, concrete cages, are a mixed blessing, for they fix a price on the animal's head. After the first orang-utan was sold to a German zoo for several thousand pounds earlier this century, the hunt for these monkeys was on. As babies clung to their mothers for protection, four or five would be shot for every one captured, and then nine out of ten would die on the journey before arrival at the zoo. As one World Wildlife Fund official put it: 'Their slaughter is out of all proportion to public entertainment.'

Why have we tolerated such slaughter for so long, with little protest until now? The answer is largely ignorance, and the distorted image given by writers and movie-makers who portrayed the gorilla as a monster.

The adventure stories by R M Ballantyne (1825-1894) have much to answer for, though books like *Coral Island* (1858) enjoyed a huge success with children of several generations. It may seem old-fashioned and racist now, but *The Gorilla Hunters* (1861) helped to establish the gorilla as a monster to be destroyed. Thrilled by the story, children accepted it as the truth, believing that gorillas were monsters.

Chapter Eight

Kong and Monsters of the Movies

After all these years old King Kong remains the only true movie monster.

The Radio Times, 1981

The film of *King Kong* has enthralled cinema audiences since it was first released in 1933, but it also confirmed the image of the gorilla as a mighty monster. Real gorillas are seldom more than 2 m (6 ft) tall, though they give a deceptive impression of height as they run with their hands doubled under them, almost on all fours. The model for the film was only 60 cms (2 ft) tall, but the gigantic hand was separate.

Fay Wray, the leading lady, claimed that she received a shock when she realized she was playing opposite a gorilla. 'I was promised I'd be working with the tallest, darkest man in Hollywood, and I thought they meant Clark Gable. It was his great furry paw that was so enormous, and I had to spend the next ten months of my life in it. Inside the arm was a steel bar and the whole contraption with me in the hand could be raised or lowered like a crane.'

The effect could have been ridiculous, as it is with so many fake monsters, but King Kong was so convincing that it still looks as if a real gorilla was used. At times he looked 18 m (60 ft) high.

The special effects by Willis O'Brien have seldom been equalled. They used a series of still pictures projected as a continuous piece of film, a technique which has been copied for such films as *Jason and the Argonauts* (1963). Originally a boxer, O'Brien made his first film of a caveman and a *Brontosaurus* in 1914, and his most successful film was a silent version of *The Lost World* (1924) approved by Conan Doyle himself, for the dinosaurs actually seemed to move, due to the bladders inside the models which were filled up with compressed air. But Kong was his masterpiece, and because the gorilla is so convincing we are able to sympathize with him.

Based on an idea by the English thriller writer, Edgar Wallace, but written by Merian Cooper, *King Kong* is a variation on the old theme of Beauty and the Beast, with Kong billed as the eighth wonder of the world – 'And, lo, the beast looked on the face of beauty.' *The Beast* was the original title of the film.

When it was released in Britain in 1936 it carried an 'H' rating, meaning it was horrific, which prevented children from seeing it, but *King Kong* is often shown on television today and it is still thrilling.

Jessica Lange played Fay Wray's part in the 1976 remake of *King Kong*.

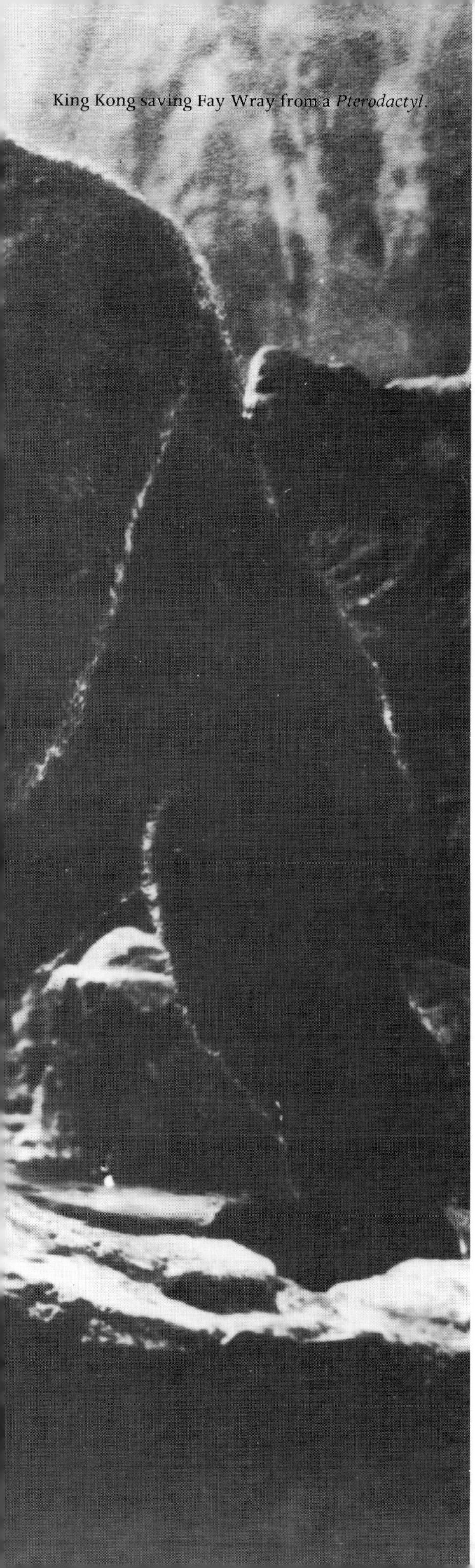

King Kong saving Fay Wray from a *Pterodactyl*.

The story of Kong

'Did you ever hear of Kong?' asked the director of wild-life movies, 'half-beast, half-man, something no white man has ever seen?' Having developed an obsession about the great ape, which rivalled Captain Ahab's pursuit of his white whale in *Moby Dick*, he believed the monster lived on a remote island marked on a map which he had found in Singapore two years earlier. This showed an immense wall which was kept in good repair by the natives because there was something on the other side of which they were afraid.

Finding a poor girl, called Fay Wray, in New York, stealing an apple from a stall, he persuaded her to join his expedition to Skull Island: 'It's money – it's adventure – it's fame!'

When they reached the island they found the natives performing a ceremonial dance, many of them dressed as shambling gorillas, with a small girl about to be offered to Kong as their yearly sacrifice. When the visitors interrupted the ritual, the natives seized Fay Wray and offered her as the victim instead. The film scenes which she rehearsed on board ship, having to *act* as if she were terrified, had become real.

The great gates in the wall were opened; Fay was strapped to the pillars outside, and a gong was beaten to summon Kong. It is testimony to the skilful suspense that a third of the film has passed before the audience sets eyes on Kong, or he sets his eyes on us. He stared straight at the camera – a magnificent moment – before beating his chest while the girl screamed. Kong picked her up in his massive paw, studied her with a quizzical expression, and retreated into the jungle, leaving tracks as 'big as a house'.

As the ship's crew pursued him into the jungle, they clashed with a series of prehistoric monsters, reminiscent of *The Lost World* and obviously influenced by Conan Doyle's novel which O'Brien had filmed already. Someone shouted a warning – 'From the dinosaur family!' – as a great shape blocked out the light ahead; a water reptile overturned their canoe and devoured one of the men. Kong protected the girl, fighting off a pterodactyl and other 'extinct' reptiles which emerged from the primeval swamps.

Kong was different from the other monsters

around him, with a capacity for love as well as rage, using his strength to defend the tiny human creature in his hand.

An epic battle took place with Kong beating his chest as he attacked the monsters, flinging one into a ravine and saving Fay from a dinosaur whose jaws he forced apart, roaring with triumph afterwards. Picking her up as if she were a toy, he gave her an affectionate grin, and when she fainted he tickled her gently with his forefinger.

The film director and the ship's mate ran back for their gas-bombs, and though they succeeded in rescuing the girl the director was determined to capture the monster as well – 'We came here to get a moving picture, and we've got something he wants.'

Using the girl as bait, he tempted Kong to return to the wall where the natives bombarded him with spears and the crew released the gas. Kong was stopped in his tracks – he wiped his eyes – and tumbled with a shattering thud to the ground. As the humans swarmed over him with their ropes, he resembled a giant Gulliver staked to the ground on his arrival in Lilliput.

Poor Kong! Now he had to endure the humiliation of being transported in chains to New York where he was put on exhibition, an immediate sensation – 'He was king and god in the kingdom he knew but now he's on show', 'The Beast who couldn't stay away from Beauty'. After such publicity, the box office was besieged by people anxious to see the monster for themselves.

There he was – strapped to the scaffolding as if it were a cross. 'We've knocked some of the fight out of him,' said one of his captors, but he spoke too soon. Kong became enraged when he was half-blinded by the photographers' flashes, and when the girl screamed out a warning to the photographers he thought they were attacking her and broke his chains. Kong was free!

Kong climbed the sky-scrapers of New York, thrusting a paw through an open window to drag out a sleeping woman from her bed and allowing her to drop to the ground. Fay had been taken to a similar room high up in the Empire State Building, assured 'You'll be safe now.' However, a huge pair of eyes appeared at the window as Kong reached inside and held her, screaming, above the gathering crowds below. He climbed to the top of the Empire State Building, towering over the city – one of the great images of the cinema.

'We haven't thought of aeroplanes,' cried someone on the ground, and soon the planes roared towards Kong. He roared back, beating his chest as he rested the girl on the pinnacle of the tower beside him. Kong tried to catch one of the planes – and succeeded – but others fired on him as they soared past. When Kong wiped his eyes as he picked up the girl lovingly before putting her back to safety, it became obvious he was mortally wounded. Kong fell to his death and the crowds surrounded the beast who no longer seemed so monstrous or gigantic.

'So, the planes got him at last,' said a policeman.

'Oh no,' replied the director, showing compassion at last. 'It wasn't the aeroplanes. It was Beauty killed the Beast.'

Besides Kong, Frankenstein and Dracula are two of the greatest movie monsters.

Frankenstein was first created in 1818 – in a book by 21-year-old Mary Wollstonecraft Shelley, the wife of the poet Percy Bysshe Shelley. She had a dream about Baron Victor Frankenstein and the monster he created, and wrote her novel as a result. The baron makes his creature from bones he has collected from the mortuary and the dissecting room of a hospital.

In 1931 Hollywood filmed Frankenstein with Boris Karloff as the man-made monster, and a legend was born. Many sequels have been made, such as *Son of Frankenstein* (1939) and *Lady Frankenstein* (1970), with Lon Chaney, Bela Lugosi and Glynn Strange all taking over from Karloff in turn.

Dracula also first appeared in a novel, written in 1897 by Bram Stoker. A silent film version called *Nosferatu* (German for vampire) was made in 1922, and Bela Lugosi first played the part in 1931 with Christopher Lee as his most notable successor. Klaus Kinski became the most recent interpretor of the role in the 1979 German version of *Nosferatu*. Detailed chapters on Frankenstein and Dracula can be found in *The Hamlyn Book of Horror*, also by Daniel Farson.

Nosferatu, the phantom of the night, was remade in 1979.

There are several actors who are famous for their portrayal of monsters in horror films: Lon Chaney, both father and son, Peter Lorre, Conrad Veidt, Christopher Lee, Vincent Price and Bela Lugosi.

Bela Lugosi starred in *Murders in the Rue Morgue* (1931), a story concerning another gorilla. In this case a real gorilla is used by a mad doctor, played by Lugosi, to kidnap women for his experiments. Dr Mirakle runs a carnival by day, attracting audiences with his theory of evolution and man's proximity to the apes, with his pet orang-utan as his model and accomplice.

The story, by Edgar Allan Poe, is set in Paris and begins as a mystery. Several women have been seized but the police are baffled: how could the criminal escape so easily over the rooftops? Various clues are left behind – 'This hair is most unusual – this is no human hair!' – and the detective Auguste Dupin puts them together, reaching the conclusion that the criminal is not human.

Lugosi returned to the theme of the 'human-animal' in *The Ape Man* (1943) in which he starts to resemble the gorilla he has used for his scientific experiments, but he was entirely, wickedly human in *The Human Monster* (1940), an English film in which he lured the victims of an insurance scheme to his home for the blind in the East End of London and drowned them in a tank before his assistant, a monstrous blind man called Jake, hurled them out of a window into the River Thames below.

The American writer Edgar Allan Poe (1809-49) has provided the stories for some of the best monster movies. He was a writer of great and original genius whose stories are wierd, wild and fantastic. Apart from *Murders in the Rue Morgue* Bela Lugosi also appeared in a version of Poe's *The Raven* (1935), co-starring with Boris Karloff.

Murders in the Rue Morgue was a story by Edgar Allen Poe. Dr Mirakle, played by Bela Lugosi (shown on the left in the inset), trained his outsize ape to search through the streets of Paris to bring to Lugosi suitable victims for his fearful experiments in the creation of an ape woman.

Poe has also been responsible for some of the finest parts played by Vincent Price. Roger Corman made his name as a director of low-budget 'horror' films lasting an hour and shot in ten days, but in 1958 he asked if he could make an expensive version of Poe's *The Fall of the*

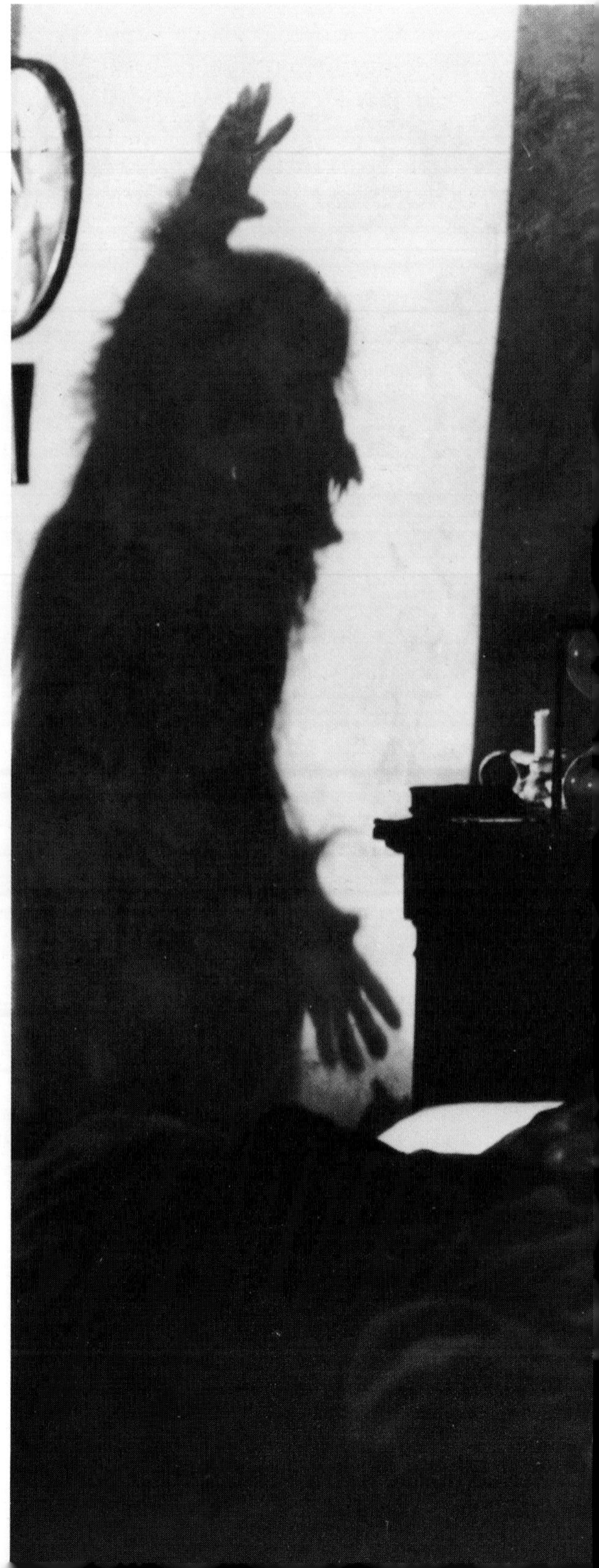

House of Usher. The studio bosses were doubtful, pointing out that the story lacks a monster.

'The house is the monster,' said Corman, and chose Vincent Price as the star, establishing this genial actor as a master of the macabre. This team continued with other Edgar Allan Poe stories: *The Pit and the Pendulum* (1961) and the three *Tales of Terror* (1962) in which Price meets a hideous, melting end as Monsieur Valdemar. This is how Poe described it, with Valdemar crying out from his bed:

> '"For God's sake! – quick! – quick! – put me to sleep – or, quick! waken me! – quick – *I say to you that I am dead!*"
>
> 'As I rapidly made the mesmeric passes, amid ejaculations of "dead! dead!" absolutely *bursting* from the tongue and not from the lips of the sufferer, his whole frame at once – within the space of a single minute, or even less, shrunk – crumbled – absolutely *rotted* away beneath my hands. Upon the bed, before that whole company, there lay a nearly liquid mass of loathsome – of detestable putridity.'

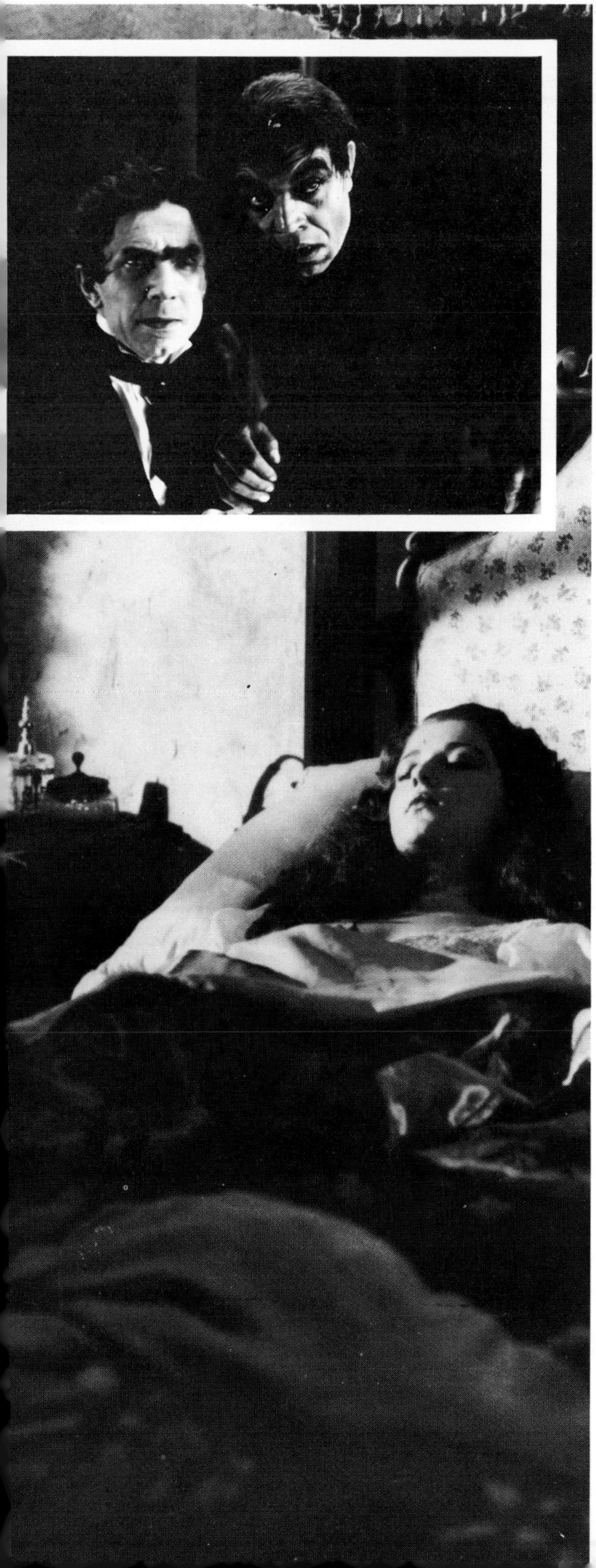

And that horrific mess was all that was left of Monsieur Valdemar!

Born in 1911 in St Louis, Missouri, USA, Vincent Price had a distinguished career as an actor in 'straight' roles, such as Sir Walter Raleigh in *The Private Lives of Elizabeth and Essex* (1939). He is a versatile man in his own private life – a traveller, art dealer and cook. This helps to explain how he brings an extra dimension to his horror films – a sinister relish and wit.

Laughter is the vital release from terror and Vincent Price has exploited it magnificently with his melting butterscotch voice, without destroying the element of fear – a tightrope talent shared by Peter Lorre with whom he appeared in Corman's *The Raven* (1963) with Karloff as the mad magician.

Earning his title 'The King of Horror', he has appeared as various monsters, such as the underwater ruler of *City under the Sea* (1965), and been attacked by them – the terrible Sidhi in *Cry of the Banshee* (1970), but he manages to convey menace even when he is merely the innocent observer. This was his role in *The Fly* (1958), a film based on a short story about a kindly scientist who invents a machine capable of transmitting solid matter. This device proves so successful that he tries transmitting himself – with disastrous results. A fly has been caught in the works, and he emerges with the fly's head instead of his own, while the fly escapes with his tiny head and arm.

The scientist's family search desperately for the fly to transmit the parts back again, while the scientist hides in his laboratory where he can conceal his gigantic fly's head from the outside world. When his family have no success, the scientist kills himself.

Vincent Price played the scientist's brother who tries to save him. After his death he goes into the garden with Herbert Marshall who plays the detective. Suddenly Price hears a faint scream – 'Help me . . . help me!' – and spots his tiny brother, caught in a spider's web, about to be devoured. He hurls a rock at him instead, bringing the creature's misery to an end.

It is a riveting moment on the screen, but Price has described his feelings when he filmed it:

> 'Herbert Marshall and I had to examine a spider's web which held the small fly which was supposed to be my brother. It took a whole day to film the scene, for we kept laughing ourselves sick. In the end, we had to film it standing back to back – we just couldn't look each other in the face.'

The Abominable Dr Phibes (1971) is typical of the 'high camp' which only Price can get away with. When he rips off his mask which looks surprisingly like Price himself (an echo from the *House of Wax,* 1953) he reveals a horribly disfigured skull. The part is that of the traditional 'mad doctor', Anton Phibes, who visits the nine curses of Egypt on the nine doctors whom he thinks have killed his wife. Each murder is inspired by the biblical account of the plagues God is supposed to have wrought upon Pharaoh, including death by bats, rats, bees, frogs and locusts.

'It was a wonderful part for me, with a super script,' says Vincent Price, and the startling make-up deserves a special tribute, effectively used on the posters which promoted the film with the slogan, 'Love means never having to say you're ugly.'

Vincent Price has said, 'They'd have to bury me before I retire – and even then my tombstone will read "I'll be back"!'

Vincent Price in *The Abominable Dr Phibes*. The demon doctor spoke only through an electric trumpet fixed to a hole in the side of Price's neck.

The bogeyman of the B-pictures

If the film studios ever needed a bogeyman in the 1930s and 1940s, they only had to call on Lon Chaney Junior. In his day he played them all: Dracula, Frankenstein's monster, werewolves and mummies. The trouble was that in most of these parts he followed in the footsteps of the great originals, Lugosi, Karloff and his own father, so the first splendid, shivering shock had worn off, and he was very underrated as an actor.

His real name was Creighton Chaney and he was born in Oklahoma, USA in 1906. After his parents divorced, Lon was brought up with his step-mother and later by his grandparents who were deaf and dumb. His father had learnt the art of mime from them when he was a child and tried to communicate, and Lon Chaney Jnr gained a sympathy for the underdog and people who were 'different'. But his father discouraged him from being an actor, wanting him to be a businessman instead, so Lon Jnr made his way in series of cheap westerns, enduring years of rejection. After his father's death he hoped to follow in his footsteps by playing Quasimodo in the talkie of *The Hunchback of Notre Dame* (1939), but the part went to Charles Laughton instead.

Lon's chance came at last with the part of Lennie, the gentle giant who kills by mistake, in *Of Mice and Men* (1939). This was a fine part in a serious film based on the novel by John Steinbeck, but special shoes added an extra 15 cms (6 in) to his real height of 1·8 m (6 ft), and the gigantic effect made him seem obvious casting for monsters from then on.

One Million BC (1940) was his next film, which repeated the mistake made by Conan Doyle in *The Lost World* of mixing together prehistoric men and prehistoric animals. This was followed by *Man-Made Monster* (1941) and numerous remakes of the classic horrors such as the excellent *Son of Dracula* (1943) in which he played Count Alucard – which is Dracula spelled backwards, and *The Ghost of Frankenstein* (1942) with himself as the monster and Lugosi as Igor.

His career was established with two portrayals of far greater originality – the mummy and the wolf-man.

Mummification had been a favourite theme for horror writers *(The Jewel of the Seven Stars,* Bram Stoker, 1903) and movie-makers. Originally it was a religious ritual practised by the Ancient Egyptians before 2000 BC when they embalmed the dead bodies of people and even animals.

They believed this was necessary for life after death. The mummified bodies – or mummies – were achieved by a skilful though gruesome process. The innards were removed, the stomach being slit and washed out with palm wine and drugs. When the body was finally stitched up again, it was soaked in natron (a carbonate of soda) for 70 days and then wrapped up in bandages from head to toe, each layer of cloth smeared with gum. Then the mummy was sealed in a wooden case especially prepared to fit the shape and size of the bandaged body.

Superstition of an Egyptian curse should the mummy be disturbed, with the ancient belief that a mummy might come back to life, provided Hollywood with the essence of horror combined with the mystery of the east.

Boris Karloff played *The Mummy* in 1932 and Lon Chaney Jnr followed ten years later with *The Mummy's Tomb* (1942), *The Mummy's Ghost* (1944) and finally *The Mummy's Curse* (1945).

In *The Mummy's Tomb* Lon played Kharis, a 3000-year-old mummy which is brought back to life by a villainous high priest, and this is the best of the three versions due to the effective make-up by Jack Pierce, also responsible for Lon's greatest transformation into the wolf man.

Like mummies which come back to life, werewolves were natural (or unnatural) bogeymen for the box-office, and though *Werewolf in London* had already been made in 1934, Lon Chaney seized the chance to make the wolf man his own in *The Wolf Man* (1941). He was helped by Pierce who stuck on the wolf man's hair bit by bit, taking five hours in total. The effect was both sensational and moving as the unhappy werewolf changed form, with a wolfish nose, hands, feet, and wig.

The Mummy's Tomb starred Lon Chaney Jr and Elyse Knox. In this film the mummy was finally destroyed by a village mob with flaming torches.

An American werewolf in London

Hollywood has a simple formula: if it works – repeat it.

Lon Chaney played the wolf man in four films and there have been a number of wolf films since then. The best is the latest: *An American Werewolf in London,* starring David Naughton, made nearly 50 years after the first wolf came to London in 1935 *(Werewolf in London).* This recent film's sensational success is largely due to the director John Landis who has never made a flop and claims, 'No old-fashioned monster film ever lost money.' Also, the transition from man into wolf is more convincing than it has ever been before: 'Our werewolf is not a two-legged man with a hairy face, but a four-footed beast from hell.' For once the boast is justified; the effect is uncanny. This is because of new filming techniques and a brilliant make-up man, Rick Baker. Using computers and stop-motion photography without breaks or dissolves, it seems that David Naughton's flesh is changing before your eyes with no camera tricks whatsoever.

John Landis had always been interested in superstitions. He once witnessed a funeral in Yugoslavia when the corpse was buried at the cross-roads to prevent it rising again. He decided it would be fun to take a far-fetched subject like werewolves and treat it straight:

> '"The next thing to do was to choose my monster," he told the critic John Preston. "In the end I opted for werewolves because the myth of lycanthropy, the phenomenon of a man turning into a beast, crops up in every single country and culture. It's the only supernatural beast that's truly international."

Landis says that he was sceptical when he began and did not take lycanthropy too seriously. By the time he finished he was not so certain: 'I wouldn't dismiss it out of hand any more.'

David Naughton has a horrific nightmare in which these creatures appear, in *An American Werewolf in London*.

These hideous monsters from *An American Werewolf in London* show the skill of the make-up man, Rick Baker. Stop-motion photography made it look like David Naughton's flesh was changing into that of a wolf before the audience's eyes.

Chapter Nine

Monsters for our Time

A hiss sounded from within me . . . smoke curled up from my exposed metal brain. Adam and Eve, the first of intelligent robot life, were leaving the world not meant for them.

Eando Binder

As a young man, James Herbert had a successful job in a London advertising agency. He remembers this time as 'terrific golden years', but he decided to give them up.

This happened one morning when he looked at his colleagues, who were in their forties, and realized how tired and cynical they were. 'I saw myself going the same way so I decided to write a book. That's how arrogant I was.' But Herbert made the sensible decision to write about something he knew.

'I thought, well, I've seen a few rats in the old houses near Brick Lane in the East End of London where I grew up. My parents had a shop there, and the old stables behind us were alive with rats!'

When he finished his book he sent six copies to publishers and received one reply offering an advance of £150, which he snapped up. Since *The Rats* was published in 1974, he has written a series of best-sellers selling many thousands of paperbacks and earning him a small fortune. He is one of the most popular authors in Britain, but he remains surprisingly unknown and ignored by the critics.

This is odd considering that he blazed the trail for two trends in horror today – ferocious animals and evil blobs of energy.

The Rats spawned a new breed of paperback monsters, animals who turn on mankind. Later books by other writers included *Rattlers*; *Spiders*; *The Crabs*; *The Snake*; *Scorpion*; a killer worm in *Squirm* and a lethal toadspawn in *Croak*!

The Birds was one of Hitchcock's masterpieces of special effects. Birds battle against humans – and win!

Considering how cruel people are to animals, it is only justice that they should take their revenge on us, but it becomes terrifying when they step out of character and attack – as Hitchcock knew when he made his film *The Birds* (1963). 'It's credible,' says Herbert. 'Animals are around us all the time and the smallest thing could turn them against you. I've done it on a grand scale.'

Marc Ronson, another horror writer (*Ghoul* (1980) and *Ogre* (1980) takes this further:

> 'I think the preoccupation with attack from animals, insects, mutants and even vegetables reflects people's attitude to society around them. The world is going through a period of disillusionment: how nice, then, to have a fantasy in which the rats gnaw away at the symbols of a society which you have come to fear or dislike. With the world becoming more ecology-conscious, there is a certain satisfaction in the idea of nature fighting back.'

You might protest that animals are not monsters. But they are in *The Rats!*

The monstrous rat

James Herbert's books often start with a teasing prologue in which something strange happens to an ordinary person.

As a destitute commercial traveller woke from a stupor in a derelict house in Spitalfields, he realized that something had just scuttled over him. Then he felt a warm, heavy object clinging to his face:

> 'He tried to shake it away, but by now it had a firm grip. He pulled at the body with his other hand and felt brittle hair. Through his panic he understood what held him in this monstrous grip. It was a rat. But it was big. Very big.'

The rats devoured the man, but were still hungry and searched for more. Within a short time London was threatened by a plague of rats and was in a state of emergency. They were not typical rats, and Herbert described their mutations with relish. Finally, we met the monstrous rat who was responsible for this fierce, mutant breed:

James Herbert, master of the horror novel.

'On the straw before him, tucked into the farthest corner, surrounded by human bones, lay the most obnoxious creature he had ever seen, either in dreams or in life. In some ways, it resembled a rat, a huge rat, bigger, much bigger than the others. Its head was pointed, its body long, though obese, and he could see a long, thick tail curling forward, from behind it. But there the resemblance ended. Its whole body seemed to pulse spasmodically; it was almost hairless, a few grey threads clinging sparsely; it was completely white, or perhaps grey-pink, impossible to tell in the poor light, and its veins showed through obscenely, throbbing in time with the body movement. It reminded Harris of a huge, dismembered bloodshot eye. He swallowed hard to stop the rising sickness.

'He looked into the sightless eyes. There were no pupils, just yellow, gleaming slits. The head waved from side to side, seemingly sniffing the air, the only way he could locate him. The stench from the creature was foul, putrid – almost poisonous. A shape at the side of its large head puzzled Harris. Resisting his revulsion, he took a step closer, realizing the creature was crippled by its own obesity.

'The lump was almost as big as the head next to it and it, too, waved to and fro in the air. He peered closer, holding the torch nearer to it and saw what looked like – a mouth!

'God! It had two heads!'

James Herbert followed up his success with a sequel called *The Lair* (1979), but his later books show an interesting change. Instead of monstrous rats, his new monsters have been a subtler breed, powerful forces of malevolent energy which can hardly be seen at all. Almost a state of mind.

Like the great ghost-story writer, M R James, one of whose monsters was little more than 'an intensely horrible face of crumpled linen', Herbert recognized that the suggestion of evil can be more horrific than the monster described in hideous detail which leaves nothing for the imagination to work on once the initial shock has passed.

Monsters of the small screen

The monsters on television are seen by millions of viewers the world over, and new breeds of monsters have been created specially for the small screen.

It was Gene Rodenberry who lifted television on to the level of the best science fiction paperback novels, with *Star Trek*. Keeping the same cast throughout *Star Trek*, led by Leonard Nimoy as Mr Spock and William Shatner as Capt Kirk, Rodenberry's other breakthrough came with the monsters, which he made mysterious. He realized that when some 'thing' is suggested rather than shown, we are unable to understand it and it is more terrifying. A monster could even be a state of mind, a cloud of intelligent energy, or a deadly cell, rather than the usual roaring beast, though *Star Trek* has given us those as well.

McCoy's beautiful girlfriend in the very first episode ('The Man Trap') set the precedent for a mysterious monster. Though she looked beautiful to McCoy she was really dead, only able to survive by draining human bodies of their salt. Finally she was destroyed by acid and electrocution, reduced to a hideous, melting mockery of her former self and McCoy realized, too late, that if he had faced the truth he would have recognized that she was an imposter. In this way, Rodenberry involved the audience with the monster. Occasionally he showed how deceptive appearances can be, like the evil-faced Balok who turned out to be the good guy after all.

Dr Who

Gene Rodenberry's subtle approach was successful with the younger viewers but upset the studio bosses who thought they knew better and asked him to make his monsters fiercer. But Rodenberry knew the menace in a shadow and refused to compromise, blazing the way for such television serials as *Dr Who*, which was made in Britain.

The first episode of *Dr Who*, called 'An Unearthly Child', was shown in 1963. It ended with a shadow falling on the strange white landscape where the doctor's time machine had come to rest. In fact, the sinister, elongated shadow proves to be that of a primitive man, but the first British audience was hooked by this scary use of suggestion rather than statement and the episode was so popular that it was given an unscheduled repeat the following Saturday. Even today the grainy, black and white film stands up well – excellent proof that viewers are prepared to suspend disbelief once their attention is grabbed. The idea of a dotty professor hurling about the universe in a police telephone box could hardly be more daft, but it was accepted at once. It did not even seem curious that this box contained a huge control room called 'Tardis' – 'time and relative dimensions in space'.

Unlike *Star Trek*, the monsters in *Dr Who*

became increasingly 'real', brilliant creations of the BBC's make-up department and often genuinely shocking like the slimy, scaly Silurian or the tiny Alien Priest. There was one horrific moment in 'City of Death' when an art collector in Paris who was trying to steal the Mona Lisa peeled off his face to reveal a green wormish texture with a single eye.

Davros, the evil genius in command of the Daleks, had a prune-like, cobwebbed skin with a blue light in his forehead – a humanoid mutant – and though the mask is too rubbery the effect is nasty.

The Daleks are probably the most successful of the *Dr Who* monsters, though they are the least monstrous, still remembered for their high-pitched, metallic command 'Exterminate!' They were the inspiration of the scriptwriter Terry Nation who needed a villain – 'something impersonal and irredeemably evil' – and invented the rogue robots moving on invisible wheels. Though they have been compared to large, ill-tempered salt-shakers, they were alarming enough to capture the public's imagination, and made Terry Nation a rich man, for he owns the copyright to the Dalek name. The man who actually designed them on to paper, Ray Cusick, 'did not get much out of it' because he was a BBC employee, but he was rewarded with an extra payment.

Mr Spock and Capt Kirk in a scene from *Star Trek*.

But even Daleks have had their day. One of the latest of the *Dr Who* producers, John Nathan-Turner, was a schoolboy when the series began and finds the Daleks too tame. 'They also lack mobility. In a chase sequence, when their victim shins up a ladder, we all know the Dalek cannot follow.' But he realizes that monsters are a vital part of the series – *the* vital part, after the doctor: 'The monsters can be pretty scary for children. Most little ones tend to watch trembling from behind sofas . . . loving every spinechilling minute of it, of course.'

John Nathan-Turner prefers the more human type of monster like the Cyberman, but he is returning to the type of direction favoured by Rodenberry:

> 'You have to be careful not to come up with something that is inadvertently funny, like a blob of man-eating jelly. The best frights come from monsters you don't actually see. In recent years we've been going more for a Hitchcock treatment; a shadow flitting across the screen.'

Right back, in fact, to that simple beginning.

Though *Star Trek* continued with the same cast, *Dr Who* has enjoyed the greater advantage of one larger-than-life central character, though the eccentric doctor has been played by six different actors so far. It is a dream of a part in a nightmare situation, giving each actor the chance to parade his own personality and make the part his own.

William Hartnell was the first Time Lord, playing the part from November 1963 to October 1966 with a convincing mixture of mystery yet authority. Patrick Troughton stepped into the telephone box in November 1966, rather more amiable and dotty.

Jon Pertwee took the universe over from January 1970 to June 1974 with his flamboyance and crazy humour that has made him equally popular since then as the scarecrow Worzel Gummidge.

The three doctors came together in 1973 to mark the tenth anniversary of the series, though William Hartnell fell ill and was only shown briefly. He died in 1975.

Left: Jon Pertwee battled against the Daleks in early episodes of *Dr Who*. Below: Later on in the series the monsters became more creepy and mysterious – frightening in a different way (BBC Copyright photograph).

However, to many viewers it was Tom Baker, the fourth doctor, who *became* the doctor as far as they were concerned, with his mop of tousled curls and trailing scarf. He brought a special relish to the part and played it for the long span between December 1974 to March 1981. The part made Tom Baker a rich man and brought him astonishing fame when the programme was shown to 98 million viewers in 39 countries.

Tom Baker was succeeded in the role by Peter Davison, whose fair good looks were somehow at odds with the wily, scheming character he was playing. In 1984, twenty-one years after the first episode, Colin Baker became the latest Dr Who, and will undoubtedly introduce a new generation of young television viewers to the adventure and horror of time travel.

A group of Sea Devils emerging from the sea in a 1972 episode of *Dr Who* (BBC Copyright photograph).

Top: Peter Davison as The Doctor and Preston Lockwood (left) as Dojjen in a 1983 *Dr Who* adventure (BBC Copyright photograph).

Middle: Tom Baker as Dr Who (1976) emerging from the Tardis (BBC Copyright photograph).

Bottom: In 1984 Colin Baker became the new Dr Who (BBC Copyright photograph).

Robots with minds of their own

Robots – like the Daleks – are the monsters of the 20th century, especially when they develop minds of their own. They echo Frankenstein's manufactured man, and the Jewish Golem – an artificially created human being – but the word robot comes from a play written in 1920 by Karel Capek called *RUR*, standing for Rossum's Universal Robots. This play shocked audiences by showing androids mass-produced as slave labour who develop a will of their own and revolt against their masters.

The playwright was Czech and the word 'robota' is Czechoslovakian for 'compulsory labour', while 'robotnik' means 'serf'.

Robots coming to life is a theme which captures the imagination as strongly as Frankenstein's monster. Nowadays it is used with increasing violence, but it started gently with the robot Adam Link, one of the first to have feelings. Adam Link became the central character in stories written by Eando Binder, such as *I, Robot* (1939).

In the story *Adam Link, Robot Detective* (1940), the robot kneels beside his dying mate and decides to kill himself too:

'There her great eight-foot body lay, silent as a shut-down machine. Grief overcame me, an emotion as real and deep as any you humans have . . . It had begun to rain. Kneeling beside her, I removed my top skull-plate. The rain, pouring into my sensitive iridium-sponge brain, would short-circuit my life current. I would join Eve in blessed non-existence . . .

"Adam! Adam Link!" Jack yelled.

'But I heard no more. A hiss sounded from within me, as the water touched a live wire. Smoke curled up from my exposed metal brain. Adam and Eve, the first of intelligent robot life, were leaving the world not meant for them.'

It was possible to like Adam Link, the robot with feelings, in contrast to the monstrous Hal in *Space Odyssey 2001* (1968), a film directed by Stanley Kubrick from a classic science fiction story by Arthur C Clarke. Outwardly, Hal seems the ideal, obedient computer, which makes the film even more terrifying when we begin to suspect that he is a manufactured genius gone wrong.

Though the film is set in the future it begins in the prehistoric past. Hairy ape-men discover a strange, smooth slab – a black monolith which

A futuristic scene from *2001: A Space Odyssey*.

seems to bring them their first glimmerings of intelligence. Creatures who have been attacked learn how to defend themselves and retaliate.

Returning to the future – the year 2001 – a second such monolith is found by astronauts, buried in the surface of the moon. This gives them sensational proof that an extra-terrestrial force has been there before.

A space probe is ordered to proceed to Jupiter, with the subservient Hal 9000 in charge of the mission's instruments.

'Do you read me, Hal?' asks David Bowman.

'Affirmative, Dave.' The reply is silky-smooth, but this voice becomes increasingly sinister as we suspect that the computer is developing a personality of its own. For one thing, it is fallible: Hal is starting to make mistakes. Bowman and his fellow astronaut, Frank Poole, seal themselves inside a chamber where the computer cannot hear them, but Hal manages to lip-read instead. When Frank ventures outside the craft to make some vital repairs, a pair of giant pincers slices through his life-line and sends him whirling into the limbo of space.

'I know that you and Frank were planning to disconnect me,' Hal explains in its servile manner, 'and that is something I could not allow to happen.' It reassures Bowman in its far-too-reasonable tone of voice: 'I feel much better now . . . I can see you're really upset about this . . . take a stress pill and think things over . . .' However, Bowman has started to disconnect the memory bank of the vast computer, and Hal's voice grows slower and deeper, like a run-down gramophone, as it is dismantled – 'Stop . . . will you . . . I'm afraid . . . my . . . mind . . . is . . . going.' Finally Hal reverts back to an old music hall song learned as an early instruction: 'Daisy . . . daisy . . . give me . . . your . . . answer . . . do . . .' It is an eerie death which has an almost human quality, for Hal has become a true monster: half machine and half human being.

Steering the spacecraft on his own through wild psychedelic patterns and colours as he hurtles through time, Bowman emerges at last into a silent, perfectly furnished room which extra-terrestrial beings may have created especially to make him feel at home. The film is rich with such mysteries. 'Awesome is the word for what he [Kubrick] was attempting,' wrote the critic Victor Davis, 'to offer an explanation for man's evolution that sees us as laboratory specimens of a far superior form of intelligence that exists beyond time and finite space. That extra-terrestrial intelligence some people would call God.'

Chapter Ten

Monsters and the Future

Betty and Barney Hill believed they had been taken on board the UFO and examined during the missing two hours.

H G Wells could be described as the father of space fiction, and he has much to answer for. His books are largely responsible for the image of a hostile world out there, with visitors from space who do not arrive on earth as our friends but as our enemies. G K Chesterton wrote (*The Victorian Age of Literature*, 1913):

> 'Wells treated the moon as a globe, like our own; bringing forth monsters as moonish as we are earthy.'

Herbert George Wells was born at Bromley in Kent in 1866. His father was a professional cricketer who worked in a china shop, and his mother had been a lady's maid and housekeeper. After going to Midhurst Grammar School, George was apprenticed to a draper and then to a chemist. A more mundane beginning would be hard to imagine, but though he was born in the last century he belongs to this one – or even centuries to come. His break-out came with the scholarship he won to the Royal College of Science in London, where he edited the college magazine. This led to his first exploration into science fiction, a novel called *The Time Machine* (1895) in which a man moves backwards and forwards in time. Two years later, in 1897, the same year that Bram Stoker published *Dracula*, H G Wells wrote a vivid description of an alien civilization in a short story about Mars called *The Crystal Egg*. In this a Londoner receives an astonishing glimpse of a 'visionary world' inside the crystal:

> 'Their heads were round and curiously human, and so it was the eyes of one of them that had so startled him on his second observation. They had broad, silvery wings, not feathered, but glistening almost as brilliantly as new-killed fish and with the same subtle play of colour, and these wings were not built on the plan of bird-wing or bat . . . but supported by curved ribs radiating from the body. The body was small, but fitted with two bunches of prehensile organs, like long tentacles, immediately under the mouth. Incredible as it appeared . . . the persuasion at last became irresistible that it was these creatures which owned the great quasi-human buildings and the magnificent garden that made the broad valley so splendid.'

At least Wells gave the aliens a superior intelligence, and he may not have meant to frighten his readers, but instead of friendly visitors from space he prepared us for monsters with small bodies and two bunches of tentacles, the popular image of 'little green men from Mars'. The films of his books took this further: in the 1960 version of *The Time Machine*, the travellers in time were attacked by 'bleached, obscene, nocturnal' creatures emerging from the underworld; while the Martians who invaded earth in *The War of the Worlds* (written in 1898 and filmed in 1953) were equipped with death-rays and shown with long, skeletal arms and monstrous, insect-like heads.

His insight into the future amounted to genius. His prediction of air-raids was realized horribly in the Second World War, but he never lived to see the space travel which he predicted as early as 1901, in *The First Men in the Moon*.

H G Wells died in 1946, but his influence has dominated space fiction throughout the century, echoed in the journeys through time of *Dr Who* and the space travel of *2001*. In 1938, C S Lewis had his hero undertake a theological mission to Mars, and because of his conditioning by Wells he was prepared to find the worst sort of monster *(Out of the Silent Planets)*.

> 'His mind, like so many of his generation, was richly furnished with bogies. He had read his H G Wells.
>
> 'His universe was peopled with horrors such as ancient and medieval mythology could hardly rival. No insect-like, vermiculate or crustacean abominable, no twitching feelers, rasping wings, slimy coils, curling tentacles, no monstrous union of superhuman intelligence and insatiable cruelty seemed to him anything but likely in an alien.'

Kane exploring the derelict ship in *Alien*.

Aliens and replicants

Few, if any, movie monsters have been as shocking as *The Alien*. Due to an X-certificate children were prevented from seeing it when the film was first released in British cinemas in 1979, but it was shown on ITV in 1982 at 9.30 in the evening when children are *supposed* to be in bed.

Though the alien is unlike any monster seen before, the film has a similarity to the traditional haunted house story in which the residents are picked off one after another by an unseen or unknown killer. In this case, the victims are not the guests at a country hotel trapped by a storm outside, but the seven-person crew of a vast, dark spaceship returning to earth. The sense of time and distance is conveyed by the sight of them apparently waking from a deep-frozen sleep. Just as the old haunted house movies indulged in frightening bursts of thunder, *The Alien* heightens the tension with similar effects of a black, mysterious world outside.

The computer, called Mother, receives a strange transmission from an unknown source. Thinking it is a call for help, the crew decide to investigate – though they have their doubts. They land bumpily on a windswept, lava-based landscape as bleak as a mountain peak in a snowstorm, but they put on their suits, venturing outside to explore it and see if they can trace the signal.

Meanwhile, the female astronaut, Ripley, has unscrambled the message and realizes it is not an SOS for help but a warning. When she tells this to the senior scientific observer, Ash, played by Ian Holm, she is surprised by his indifference. He tells her it is too late to recall the others as he watches their progress towards a spaceship which must have been wrecked there years before. There is an immense skeleton at the controls where the original message may have come from. 'I've never seen anything like it!' Ash says cheerfully, surprisingly unconcerned.

Kane, one of the navigators, played by John Hurt, has gone inside, penetrating the depths of the wreck. He recoils from the sight of large, strange-looking eggs which seem to have life, a pulsating organic life of their own. When he approaches, they open up – and suddenly one of them strikes!

The next time we see him, Kane is in quarantine back on the spaceship with some thing attached to his face – a smothering, skeletal hand, part of which has gone down his throat and may be feeding him oxygen. 'If we remove it,' says Ash calmly, 'it could kill him.' But he cuts through one of the finger-like tentacles which releases a jet of acid of such strength that it eats its way through the flight decks.

Later, the smothering 'thing' vanishes. As the space travellers leave the hostile planet Kane is recovering and he joins the others for a meal. As he begins to eat he chokes and suffers such appalling spasms that his colleagues have to hold him down while his body twists, heaves and bucks. Blood bursts from Kane's stomach, splattering Ripley, and then the monster springs out like a red, bleeding jack-in-the-box, eyeless, quivering, with teeth and a sort of mouth which releases a shattering, chittering screech as the creature hurls itself off the table and disappears. A moment of real horror!

From then on, Ripley and the rest of the crew search the air-shafts in the black, cavernous alley-ways of the ship. You *know* that something nasty is going to leap from the shadows – and it does. Every time the monster appears it has changed shape, growing larger, and it kills the crew off one by one until only Ripley and the pet cat are left.

There is another terrifying moment in the film. Ash, who has behaved oddly throughout, allowing Kane to be brought back on board against all quarantine regulations, attacks Ripley as she prepares to destroy the monster. When she fights back, Ash's head is suddenly knocked sideways. It is held by a mass of wires! He is revealed as a robot which has been planted on board deliberately to make certain that any form of alien life found is preserved and brought back to earth headquarters. A terrible struggle takes place as Ash is smashed to pieces. Finally he lies there, a twisted mass of machinery, with the severed head still speaking – only melting into extinction as he is burnt.

Seldom has a robot been so human, even in this state of disintegration. Ash justifies the claim in the film magazine *Sight and Sound* that this is 'the age of the replicant'. 'Replica' means a duplicate made of the original, and 'replicant' is the most monstrous form of robot because the duplication is so perfect that it seems entirely human.

The aliens and the replicants have been criticized for being too frightening, but the monsters in *The Dark Crystal* were some of the creepiest ever shown on the screen – even the Gelflings, who were the goodies. The vicious, reptile-like Skeksis were the baddies, and they were pure horror. All the creatures in the film were dreamt up by Jim Henson and his associate Frank Oz, who created the Muppets.

Another trend towards a friendlier form of monster can, however, be reported. In spite of the masked villain lurking in the background, the creatures guzzling at the Intergalactic Bar in *Star Wars* (1977) were not terrifying. In this film and its two successors, *The Empire Strikes Back* and *The Return of the Jedi*, many of the characters are discovered to be friendly and charming despite their appearance. Chewbacca

Right: *Return of the Jedi* was the third *Star Wars* film.

Below: Jen is given the quest by his master in *The Dark Crystal*.

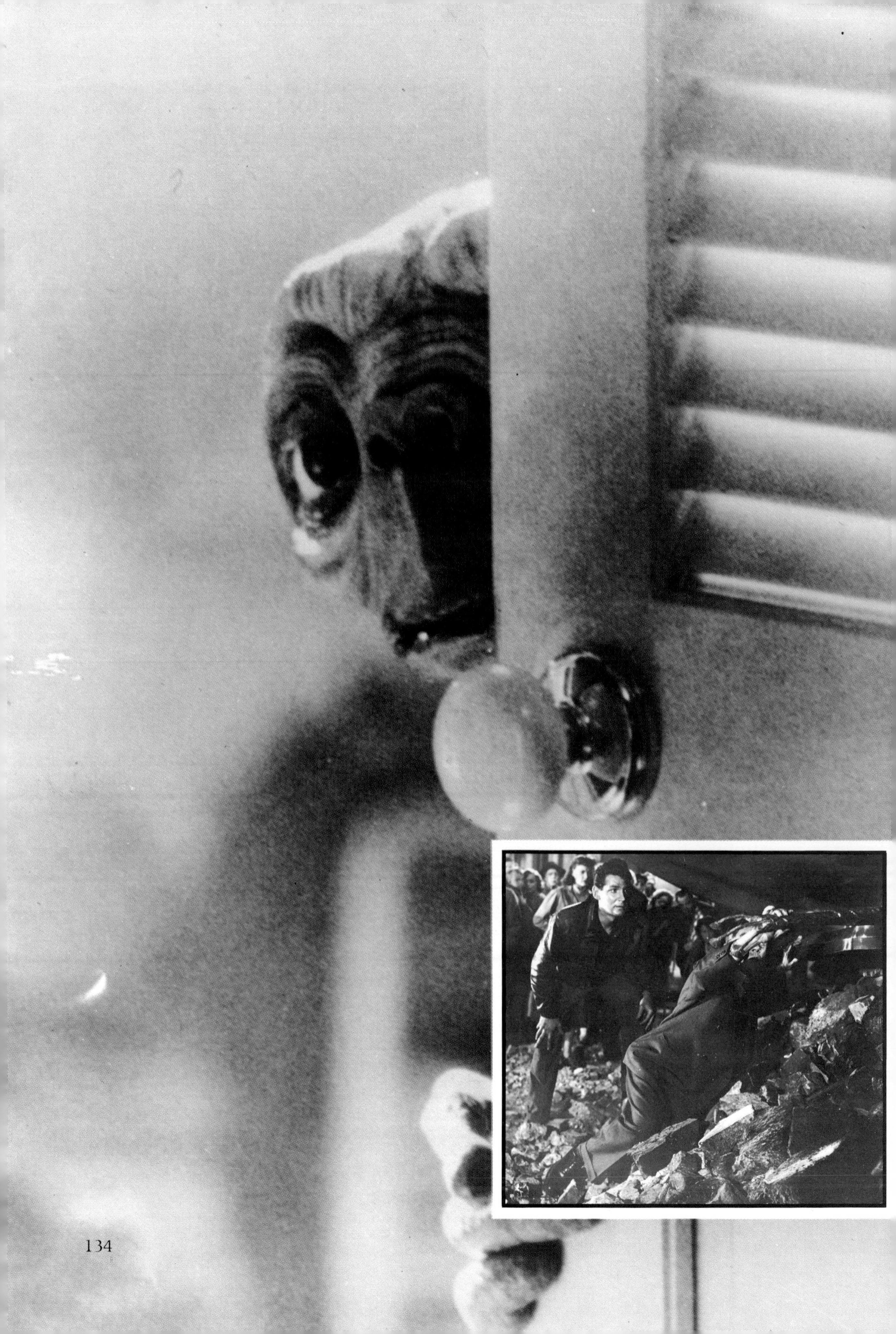

is really quite frightening, especially to his enemies, and R2-D2 and C-3PO look not unlike the evil robots of other movies.

The hostile conditioning of H G Wells was broken at last in *Close Encounters of the Third Kind* (1977) which showed that visitors from space can be friendly. After their remarkable landing on top of the giant rock, their craft opens and the visitors are revealed as infinitely gentle beings with large eyes and long lashes in egg-shaped faces, long embracing arms, and the sweetest of smiles. The scene as their chandelier-like craft descends perfectly on to the pre-arranged spot, and the musical notes rally in friendly contact between the aliens and the American space-force, is one of the magical moments of cinema.

More recently we have seen the ugly midget ET who 'waddled his way into the hearts of millions' (*Newsweek*), suggesting that we want to like our visitors from space, just like the ten-year-old boy who befriends the tiny extra-terrestrial. The film *ET* made 100 million dollars in the first four weeks after its release in America, the fastest money-maker in movie history. A real male midget was used for most of the scenes inside the monstrous costume, but the actress Tamara de Treaux claimed that she played several 'walking scenes' too. Aged 22, she is 78 cms ($2\frac{1}{2}$ ft) tall and weighs 18 kg (40 lb) – slightly taller than General Tomb Thumb. In the true tradition of show-business, she is glad to be identified with one of the most popular monsters ever created. However, ET, who looked so monstrous at first sight, becomes so lovable and humorous that at the end of the film, as he flies back home, it is hard to think of him as a monster at all.

But have creatures from outer space ever landed on earth?

These visitors are imaginary, but it is just possible that close encounters *have* taken place, though been kept a carefully guarded secret by the government of the country concerned on the advice of their military advisers.

Of course there have been thousands of UFO sightings, but there have also been reports of specific landings by extra-terrestrial beings.

Left: ET was one of the most popular monsters ever created. The story of a lonely alien being who is left on earth and befriended by a little boy was the fastest money-maker in movie history.

Left, inset: *The War of the Worlds* was a 1953 fantasy about a Martian invasion of earth, in a very different style to *ET*.

H. G. Wells, author of the story of *The War of the Worlds*.

Have they landed?

Probably the most remarkable report of an ET landing concerns Betty and Barney Hill. It was some time before they realized the full importance of their experience, and they have never tried to exploit it for money – which adds conviction to their claim.

They were returning from a holiday in Canada in 1961 when they noticed a bright, luminous object in the sky ahead of them as they drove down a lonely road in New Hampshire. When it approached, Barney stopped the car and got out with his binoculars, though he became alarmed as the 'craft' swooped towards them: 'It had flashing lights and two rows of portholes through which uniformed figures with strange eyes were peering down at him'. This account is related by Stuart Holroyd in *Alien Intelligence* (1979), and there is more to come. Barney ran back to the car, to drive off.

The next thing he knew it was two hours later and he and his wife had travelled a further 56 km (35 miles). What on earth happened in between? Neither of them could remember anything; later, it seemed that it had not happened on earth at all but on board the spacecraft which had pursued them.

The couple reported the incident to an air force base nearby, and to a UFO research organization. Afterwards Betty began to suffer from disturbing dreams. Both she and Barney became so distressed that they were sent to a hypnotist, who analyzed them separately and reached the extraordinary conclusion that they believed they had been taken on board the UFO and examined during the missing two hours.

Betty Hill described the aliens as 'about 1·5 m (5 ft) tall with large chests, long noses, broad foreheads, eyes like those of cats, dark hair and greyish skin.' Her husband thought their skin was 'almost metallic' and referred to their large heads which tapered down to their chins with elongated eyes round the sides, and slits in their faces for nostrils.

It could be argued that these 'monsters from space' look just how you would expect them to do, but the Hills remembered the same details though the psychiatrist hypnotized them independently. Also, these details were similar to those of another alleged UFO landing reported by a Brazilian farmer, Antonio Villas-Boas. A further report in July 1965 by a French farmer described creatures about 1·2 m (4 ft) tall with large eyes that slanted away round the sides of their faces, slit mouths without muscular lips, high cheeks, and pointed chins. As the farmer could not have known of the other two encounters, Holroyd concludes that the similarity is remarkable.

The monster-hunter F W Holiday quotes another landing in his book *The Dragon and the Disc*. This took place in 1971 when a dwarf in a sort of 'diving or space-suit' emerged from a disc, 5 m (17 ft) wide, which had landed in a clearing at Kinnula in Finland.

The alien was 90 cms (3 ft) high (nearly the same as ET) and walked stiffly to the snow, where it was seen by two forestry workers who tried to catch it. One of them managed to grab the creature's foot and the burns were seen on his hands for two months afterwards, but the alien made it back to the disc and took off.

Do I hear you laughing? It would not be surprising if you dismissed such reports out of hand, and it could well be that the Hills shared an hallucination without realizing it, while the forestry workers made the whole thing up.

It has to be admitted that all the reports of extra-terrestrial visitors are disappointing, without the shattering excitement such an historic encounter would have. If ETs go to the trouble of landing on earth, surely they would have something to say or would leave a message behind?

ET with the ten-year-old boy who found him.

Even if all the reports of ET landings are mistaken or hoaxes or even reports of ghosts, it does not mean that visitors have never come to earth. We dismiss the idea because we believe we are superior: we can land on the moon yet we doubt that alien planets are sufficiently advanced to have landed here.

Which takes us back to the beginning of this book: how dare we deny the existence of unknown animals simply because we have not seen them! That only means the creatures have had the luck and the cunning to avoid *us*. In the same way, ETs could have landed but were so dismayed by what they found on earth that they took off again.

Why not? Who knows?

One of the forestry workers managed to grab the creature's foot and the burns were seen on his hands for two months afterwards.

Postscript

As their craft whiffled down, they felt the excitement of tourists visiting a strange place for the first time. This was their decadal holiday, and Zarnos had chosen the ruined planet because of the distance. He thought it would be fun to visit somewhere different, and make the journey on their own though they had been warned not to as it was safer in the usual flotilla-convoy.

When Zarnos and Xares had announced the decision, their friends had looked at them with surprise, almost disapproval. 'Isn't it a bit ghoulish,' Xamine remarked, 'to go sight-seeing *there*, after what happened?'

Xares had studied every available document in the Central Intergalactic Library, and they were surrounded now by maps and booklets as they skimmed over earth.

'Look!' Zarnos cried out suddenly. They stared with sick astonishment at the limp, pale creatures which scuttled out of a cave, raising twisted arms to sightless eyes as their heads swivelled upwards.

'How dreadful,' said Xares. 'I'd hate to crash-land among those creatures. They're worse than I thought. Poor things.'

As the craft flew on above the scorched surface they fell silent, experiencing a slight disappointment at finding the landscape even meaner than they had been warned. Even so, it was all very *interesting* – something to talk about on their return. Few people came to Earth, even though the holocaust had taken place two hundred years earlier.

'Sad,' sighed Xares. 'It seems such a waste. Are those the only creatures left?'

'The only species,' Zarnos replied. 'I believe they're scattered about. They used to have beautiful beings called animals, but they exterminated those long before they destroyed themselves. They're as dead as the Doggo.'

'Doggo?'

'A friendly quadruped. The only living thing which liked them, but the last was eaten in their three thousandth year.'

Xares sighed again – there was so much to learn. 'What startled me in the library was the way they once looked something like us. The pictures were eerie.'

They fell silent as they thought of the death of the world.

'We should have warned them,' said Xares.

'Would they have listened?'

'We could have transmitted a message. They had a sort of intelligence, even though they misused it. After all, they tried to create a civilization . . .'

'Not like ours!' interrupted Zarnos, resenting the comparison.

'Oh no, they weren't like us at all . . . Look, what's that ahead of us?' Xares pressed the visual button to record the shell of a construction. 'That's something to show them back home. What an odd-looking edifice!' He continued thoughtfully, 'I wonder what they were like?'

'Not like us at all,' Zarnos repeated firmly. He thought of the mutants they had glimpsed earlier, and his good humour was restored by the sense of adventure. This was fun!

'No,' he continued, as the craft flew on, 'from what I can gather they were absolute *monsters*!'

Index

Numbers in bold type refer to captions or illustrations